Patricia lee

S/HE DRAGON
how I found my wings

PATRICIA LEE

Copyright © 2015 Patricia Lee.

All rights reserved. No part of this book may be used or reproduced by any means, graphic, electronic, or mechanical, including photocopying, recording, taping or by any information storage retrieval system without the written permission of the publisher except in the case of brief quotations embodied in critical articles and reviews.

Balboa Press books may be ordered through booksellers or by contacting:

Balboa Press
A Division of Hay House
1663 Liberty Drive
Bloomington, IN 47403
www.balboapress.com
1 (877) 407-4847

Because of the dynamic nature of the Internet, any web addresses or links contained in this book may have changed since publication and may no longer be valid. The views expressed in this work are solely those of the author and do not necessarily reflect the views of the publisher, and the publisher hereby disclaims any responsibility for them.

The author of this book does not dispense medical advice or prescribe the use of any technique as a form of treatment for physical, emotional, or medical problems without the advice of a physician, either directly or indirectly. The intent of the author is only to offer information of a general nature to help you in your quest for emotional and spiritual well-being. In the event you use any of the information in this book for yourself, which is your constitutional right, the author and the publisher assume no responsibility for your actions.

Any people depicted in stock imagery provided by Thinkstock are models, and such images are being used for illustrative purposes only.
Certain stock imagery © Thinkstock.

Print information available on the last page.

ISBN: 978-1-5043-2824-1 (sc)
ISBN: 978-1-5043-2826-5 (hc)
ISBN: 978-1-5043-2825-8 (e)

Library of Congress Control Number: 2015902693

Balboa Press rev. date: 03/06/2015

This book is lovingly dedicated to my children Tina, Kevin and Leah.

Canst thou bind the sweet influences of Pleiades, or loose the bands of Orion? Canst thou bring forth Mozzaroth in his season? or canst thou guide Arcturus with his sons? knowest thou the ordinances of heaven? canst thou set the dominion thereof in the earth?

—Job 38:31 (KJV)

Contents

Chapter 1 Dragon Landscape 1
Chapter 2 My Mothers 4
Chapter 3 Feminine Within 9
Chapter 4 Brainwashed 14
Chapter 5 Rapture 21
Chapter 6 Her Story ~ Herstory 26
Chapter 7 Pagan God Pan 31
Chapter 8 Ever Green ~ A Story 36
Chapter 9 Emotional Wheel 38
Chapter 10 Wearing Grief ~ A Teaching 42
Chapter 11 Kundalini Dragon 46
Chapter 12 Fertility 52
Chapter 13 Serpent Sacred 58
Chapter 14 Ecstatic Dance ~ A Story 62
Chapter 15 Telepathic Relationships 64
Chapter 16 River of Life ~ A Teaching 70
Chapter 17 Wilderness Awareness 72
Chapter 18 Meditation Shores 79

Chapter 19	Gyroscope ~ Blog 2006	84
Chapter 20	Body and Soul	90
Chapter 21	Oversoul ~ Blog 2006	98
Chapter 22	Seamless Reality ~ A Teaching	105
Chapter 23	Dosewallips ~ A Story	108
Chapter 24	Sacred Sites ~ Sacred Times	111
Chapter 25	Goddess Flesh ~ A Prayer	115
Chapter 26	Circle of Life	117
Chapter 27	Winged Flight	125
Chapter 28	Caterpillar to Butterfly ~ A Journey	132
Chapter 29	Achieving and Being	134
Chapter 30	Caduceus ~ A Story	141
Chapter 31	Resilience ~ Blog 2010	144
Chapter 32	Soul Retrieval	154

Acknowledgment

I wish to acknowledge Sandra Ingerman, author and shaman, for so graciously endorsing my first published book, and my editor, A.T. Birmingham Young, for assisting me in putting layers of flesh on the bare bones of my writing.

Introduction

Over forty years ago the *language of the Sacred Feminine* took me by the hand, revealing inner pathways of right-brain intuition, and leading me through mystical passageways of dreams, visions, and archetypes. In the process of learning to dance the language of *She*, I noticed another presence on the dance floor, embracing Her with grounded logic and supporting Her with practical information. This left-brain force, *He*, thrived on detail and analysis, never feeling threatened by Her lucid ways of seeing or envious of Her "speed of light" knowing. As these two opposites practiced dance steps through honest communication and fluid coordination, something amazing happened. The tingling sensation between my shoulder blades and East/West themes in dreamtime revealed I had sprouted S/He wings— with dragon attached!

What hand
turns the kaleidoscope of my days?
What shape-shifting hand—
turning moods color to color,
pattern to pattern,
creating magical display
of revolving sets
and charging me the task
of acting within them all?

What hand

plays the music of my nights,
taking me dancing through dreamtime
and bringing me back
with riddles and magical codes,
playing tricks with reality?

About the Author

Patricia Lee has been listening to the *language of the Sacred Feminine* for over forty years. Inspired by her peaceful practice of meditation, she volunteered at a peace and justice organization and worked for eighteen years at a nonprofit serving at-risk youth and families. In 2003 she founded Community Threads to offer classes, events and concerts for the "expression, education and celebration of community." Compelled to support the global movement of Transition Towns Patricia founded Transition Woodinville in 2010. Her activity book, *Circle of Life ~ Mapping One's Story,* connected her to Native Indian Tribes in Washington State where she invited tribal members to tell their life stories by creating mandala maps. Running parallel to these outer achievements, Patricia evolved spiritually as a mystic and shaman. *S/He Dragon ~ How I Found My Wings* weaves ordinary and non-ordinary realities that describe the landscape of her life. This landscape also includes three children, four grandchildren, a vegetable garden, bike riding, hiking, dancing and building a global Light Workers network on Facebook.

> Run my dear, from anything that may not
> strengthen your precious budding wings.
>
> —Hafez

Chapter 1
Dragon Landscape

I never imagined I would find my wings. No one even told me I had wings. But there they were tingling at my shoulder blades with a mystical dragon attached, breathing intuitive feminine fire, grounding detailed masculine logic, and flying me into realms of multiple dimension. This may sound like fantasy or science fiction, but it is reality. I know. This is my story. By telling it, perhaps others will choose to find their wings.

S/He Dragon ~ How I Found My Wings reveals the story of my personal and evolving relationship with Light. My life was not always associated with Light—not in a conscious way. It took a plunge into darkness and an angel to awaken me into a new way of seeing and being. Once awakened, one can never go back to being unconscious—in the dark.

Light shape-shifts matter and evolves consciousness. My story bears witness through the *language of the Sacred Feminine*, Goddess as a force of nature, shamanic journeys, mystical encounters, deep ecology, and a relationship with Gaia. How can one's life journey have so many facets of spiritual experience and expression? In the same way that a crystal holds many sharp angles and flat surfaces and white light holds a rainbow spectrum. One need not be a spiritual master to experience Light (I capitalize Light because it saved my life twice and deserves this respect). One does need to be awake/conscious and willing to let go of trappings that keep one in unconscious darkness. A spark of Light becomes a ray and a ray becomes a beam, increasingly opening one's physical body to its divine source. This penetrating power of Light rewired my brain, altered my relationships, reorganized foods I ate, and attracted lost parts of my soul. Light shape-shifted my matter again and again, transmuting me into a new multidimensional being.

Are you, whether male or female, aware of the Sacred Feminine moving through you? Do you feel and hear Her when She rises spontaneously from the depths of your being stimulating your brain and senses? Do you trust what She has to say to the nerves and muscles of your body and can you rely on Her to steer you in the right direction? Or do you ignore Her in the fast pace of your life—a life that is on overload with outside-in information and on overdrive with too much outer-stimuli?

The Sacred Feminine (right-brain intuition) and Sacred Masculine (left-brain logic) came alive within me over a forty-year period. I tell that story in the following chapters, through worldly and otherworldly dramas, teachings, short stories, blog entries, a prayer, and a journey.

I alternate emotional, rhythmic poetry with linear prose to stimulate both left-brain and right-brain hemispheres. (*The Journal of Consciousness Studies* reports that the brain responds differently to poetry and prose and it "found evidence that poetry activates brain regions associated with introspection."
—www.redorbit.com/news/science/1112971504/effects-of-poetry-on-the-brain-101013/)

Thirty-five years ago I was forever changed when a bolt of Kundalini (a Sanskrit term meaning "serpent power") fire snapped the back of my neck. This fire threw me into new brainwave territory, instantly changing the way my brain-body functioned. Processing linear information became challenging. This physiological change caused me to avoid academia and formal training that focused on learning logical and sequential information.

As I withdrew from this outside-in way of learning I witnessed some people with professional degrees and titles who were opinionated, close-minded and unkind to others. I realized that people with IQ (mental intelligence), did not necessarily have EQ (emotional intelligence). I was on a different path, learning from inner messengers, guides, allies and teachers. Thus, my education has come from within even as I walked through various churches and spiritual groups, even as I listened to an array of motivational speakers and authors, and read numerous self-help books.

Outside-in information from authority figures, books, newspapers, radio, television, and the Internet may give one identity and success in this physical, linear dimension. Inside-out inspiration deserves equal attention and expression—inspiration that sees the whole, giving life deeper meaning. This mystical foundation, full of magic and mystery, is the way of the Sacred Feminine.

> Is meaning found
> in what we own,
> who we know,
> how much we've traveled,
> our degrees and titles?
> Or is it found through expression?
> A verb rather than a noun?

> Scientists know so much about homing in animals: Bees orient to polarized light; salamanders steer by lines of geomagnetic force; garter snakes follow scent; pigeons use the position of the sun; songbirds follow the stars. They are all drawn to a place proved to be safe by the undeniable fact of their own existence. But who has studied the essential issue: What will draw our own children back home?
>
> —Kathleen Dean Moore, *River Walking*

Chapter 2
My Mothers

Mothers play a critical role in the lives of infants and children. To be "mothered" is to be held safe, nourished, and loved. As a child I was blessed to have known two mothers.

Growing up, I was held by two different mothers. One held me on her lap, imprinting my young brain with Mother Goose nursery rhymes, the smell of new books, and a soft voice and touch; the other held me in the woods, imprinting me with sensorial stimuli of nature. On Mother's lap, I felt comfort, and in Mother Nature's woods, I felt alive. Both gave me a sense of home.

My earliest memories are standing in a crib wearing a yellow sleeper; hearing schoolchildren play in the far distance, beyond the tall fir trees; pumping my little legs on a backyard swing while singing "Red Robin" and "You Are My Sunshine;" and standing on a stool at the kitchen sink dunking glass milk bottles in soapy water, entranced by bubbles that gurgled as they multiplied. What took me out of mind and body so that I could observe myself and remember these simple moments in time? Did a magical wand flick fairy dust my way? Was a celestial song catching my ear, suspending me in time and space? What window of self-awareness opened, imprinting my memory?

I spent much of my childhood in the back woods of our home in Puyallup, Washington. In spring, I woke early to carve pathways past red-ant hills and huckleberry bushes sprouting from stumps, merrily on my way to make cozy hideaways under Douglas fir and maple trees. Stomping down bracken ferns and Oregon grape, I sculpted a kitchen, living room and bathroom. Dad's plumbing business gave me direct access to porcelain toilets, sinks, and even a bathtub, making my outdoor living space primitive, modern and fun! Using wooden boards from Dad's shop, I constructed shelves, securing them between stumps or tree branches. I filled tin cans with mud and decorated them with small pinecones, fir needles and dandelions. These ready-to-serve meals lined the shelves for imaginary guests. Garter snakes, red robins, neighboring horses, and our collie Lassie kept me company as I dressed up in play clothes, sometimes stuffing dress bodices so that it looked like I had mature breasts. (I knew my dad liked women's breasts from the John Wayne movies he watched and the covers of western books he read.)

I hung May Day baskets, filled with sweetly perfumed purple lilacs, on Grandmother's trailer door. A door that invited me into her world of Ed Sullivan variety shows, viewed on her little black and white TV; card games, dominoes, and Parcheesi; and supper consisting of fried chicken hearts, gizzards and onions accompanied by lettuce leaves dressed with lemon juice and honey. Grandmother never had much to say. She taught me to appreciate the richness of silence.

Spring was a time to watch patches of bright-green slime in the slow-moving creek; and, soon after, catch wiggly pollywogs in mason jars. It was a season of wet, green growth and new activity whose signature on the land imprinted a lasting signature on my senses.

In summer, I picked wild blackberries for one of Mom's pies that won awards at the local Grange, and weeded the strawberry patch—a most boring chore. I played "king of the mountain" with my three sisters and brother (my second brother would arrive a few years later) on dirt hills near the graying barn with chicken coop and rabbit hutches, and carefully kept my distance from the neighbor's large white goose, who liked to chase and bite little girls. At night, under all phases of moonshine, we caught flying ants to feed spiders in their webs. In fall, I felt loss as green pathways turned brown and lady ferns bent over after a season of robust, upright stance. At the same time, I marveled at brilliant red, orange, and yellow leaves on nearby maple trees. Fall was a spectacle of passing splendor—its own rite of passage.

Winter held me indoors with bustling holidays and family feasts; playing with my Tiny Tears doll, paper dolls, and pick-up sticks. I danced with my siblings to the latest tunes from popular singers, such as Elvis Presley, Ricky Nelson, Connie Francis, and Brenda Lee. If snow arrived, my siblings and I put on rubber boots, wool mittens, and hats to sled down hills on our long driveway. Building a snow fort and launching a snowball attack were part of our winter festivity.

Year round, my senses attuned to the sights, sounds, smells, tastes, textures, and motions of wet spring turning to hot summer, to dry autumn, to cold, still winter. I wasn't conscious of the magic and mystery of nature. I was simply in it, relating as an elemental child of water, fire, air, and earth.

I played under sky season after season until something changed. All of a sudden, I could no longer jump off woody stumps or run freely down dirt hills. Fear had crept in, holding me back. I was no longer carefree. Was this a self-consciousness that develops alongside one's ego personality? Was this growing up? Or was it unexpected circumstances that alter childhood innocence?

Country roads lined with fir trees provided opportunity for serene bike rides, except for one instance when the serenity was broken by a man in a truck offering candy, trying to lure me and my friend into his vehicle. I didn't know about "stranger danger," people who prey on children. My inclination (I was taught to be polite) was to talk to the man. My friend was not so polite and urged me to go. When this half-naked man started to ask me questions about his penis, I peddled away to join my friend. I was confused and bewildered. Mom called the police, and feeling as if something was wrong with me for talking to a man with his pants down, I experienced shame. My childhood had been innocent and carefree. Now, a cloud of doubt set in.

Still, Mother Nature continued to expand into my day-to-day living as an arcing feminine presence. I continued to feel safe in her earthy green and brown canopy. She was there when I turned eight and accepted Jesus as my savior, knowing him as "my hero" who healed the sick and helped the poor. Jesus, whose Bible stories struck a deep chord within—stories that would serve as background music as I meandered through life. Songs from this time continue to bubble up to consciousness, such as "I'm so happy and here's the reason why: Jesus took my burdens all away" and "This little light of mine, I'm gonna let it shine."

She was there in fifth grade as I reached out to the boy who lived in a shack, wore dirty clothes, and smelled bad. The boy others made fun of, the boy I taught to read. She was nudging me to smile at the black boy on the school bus—the first person of color I had ever seen. She was there influencing my early years by the art and heart of kindness.

Through changing seasons in the Puyallup woods and changes in my personal development, nature had been the primary relationship that fed all my senses. I smelled her wet spring and dry summer; heard her voices of wind, rain, thunder, and lightning; saw her myriad colors change; tasted her sweet berries; and felt her under my feet, over my head, and in my hands as I used her generous gifts for my creative world. She did not withhold emotion. In fact, she was a constant flow of dynamic energy-in-motion, and I enjoyed her company. I would not forget her, for I was part of her. I never thanked her in a conscious way. I did thank her by running into her arms and joyfully playing in her love.

> We're so engaged in doing things to achieve purposes of outer value that we forget that the inner value, the rapture that is associated with being alive, is what it's all about.
>
> —Joseph Campbell, *Myths & the Modern World*

CHAPTER 3
FEMININE WITHIN

Nature was a dynamic communicator. She expressed herself freely, holding nothing back. My family did not have this fluidity of expression. Feelings went unspoken leaving me without a sense of emotional identity.

Chanting, "Sitting in a grandstand, beating on a tin can, who can? We can—w*in!*" while wearing a purple sweatshirt and gold, corduroy flare skirt that Mom had sewn is a memory threading back to cheerleading days in sixth grade. In junior high and high school, I wore red every Friday (after high school I never wanted to wear red again!) and shook white crepe-paper pompoms while cheering, "Two bits, four bits, six bits, a peso, all for Franklin Pierce, stand up and say so!" I liked cheerleading. It was a way to inspire a crowd of people, instill school spirit, support the teams, dance to music, and have fun. As a high school senior, I was elected homecoming queen and wore a long, white, satin dress and silver crown. In addition to popularity, I had good grades, had an athletic, all-state football player boyfriend, and was college bound.

So how did this positive thread unravel, taking me to the bottom at age twenty-five? How did this "all together" image end up in subtraction? It did so because the image was shallow, lacking substance, and what was underneath was creating havoc. Why? Looking back at my journals this poem that I wrote in 1998, held a clue.

> Dad was a doer.
> He built me camps in the woods,
> birdhouses from Hi C juice cans,
> a glass display case for my water-cycle project,
> wooden box divided for my rock collection—
> metamorphic, igneous, sedimentary.
> He was an outdoorsman. He fished; he hunted;
> he was a volunteer—boy scouts, firefighter.
> He was a working man. Construction, plumbing, hot-water heating—
> all these things he did, yet I still don't know who he was.
> He never talked about his feelings.

As a family we never talked about feelings. Conversations revolved around surface topics that included who, what, when, and where but never the deeper nature of why someone felt or thought the way they did. Like spinning wheels, our conversations and relationships lacked traction, and I was not able to grab onto anything meaningful. Was I a "mistaken zygote" like the story of an infant who was dropped into the wrong family, as told by Clarissa Pinkola Estes in *Women Who Run with the Wolves?* Was I a misfit like the ugly duckling of fairy-tale fame?

When I was a child, we didn't have stickers with facial expressions identifying a myriad of feelings. We didn't have names for feelings, nor did we have permission to safely express them. Mom, Dad, and other adults in my world did not consciously know this terrain and were unable to offer any guidance, leaving me to drift in an emotionless void. According to researcher Aletha Solter, founder of The Aware Parenting Institute, "A child can grow up confused about their feelings and vague about their needs when their feelings are ignored, pacified, or punished." (www.parentingwithpresence.net/index.php?pageid=906)

The melodic sounds and sensual textures of expressed feelings, or "e-motions" (energy-in-motion), give voice to the Sacred Feminine that resides within every male and female. Feelings connect us soul-to-soul, giving relationships spiritual dimension. Without "feminine" feelings, my world as a child was flat. Recognizing and expressing honest feelings is the building block for mental, emotional, physical, and spiritual health.

> *It is important for caregivers to name feelings that children express, as well as providing culturally appropriate models of how to react when feeling certain emotions. These strategies provide children with the support needed to identify their own feelings and an idea of how they can express themselves while learning to better manage their growing range of emotions. The ability to express and manage emotions impacts children's emotional development and also influences how children form social relationships with others.*
> —www.illinoisearlylearning.org/guidelines/domains/domain1/emotionexp.html

The lack of honest emotional communication in my childhood left me feeling disconnected at the family dinner table. What a simple thing it would have been for Dad to have said, "I am upset today. I lost the hot-water heating job," or Mom to have said, "I am feeling tired and need some time for myself." Unspoken feelings created a chaotic underground environment that plagued my sister and me with rash on our necks and arms. Honest, healthy emotional expression was a missing link in my childhood, as it was in my parents' and their parents' childhoods. As a child of emotionless parents, I have the opportunity to change family patterns through the conscious expression of my feeling nature.

One cannot be fully aware of something until it is embodied, expressed emotionally. This is very different than knowing about something with one's analytical mind. If one wants to know happiness, express the colors and sounds of happiness. If one wants to know peace and love, express the compassionate qualities of peace and love.

A young girl or boy cannot develop a healthy and whole identity when their "feminine" half of self-expression, their feelings, are not recognized. This need for emotional recognition is not for ego's sake but for soul's sake. If a parent doesn't say through their eyes, words, and actions, "I see you" and "I hear you," how can one see, hear, and know oneself? This reflecting and mirroring is critical in our young lives at a time when self-image patterns are developing—a time when the blueprint of identity is starting to set. Without this inner feminine aspect of myself being acknowledged, I was unseen and unheard.

My parents worked hard to provide for our large family. As a child, I took ballet and tap-dance lessons, was well dressed (Mom enjoyed fashion and taught me to appreciate wardrobe color coordination), learned to sew (winning blue ribbons at the local fair), and went to Girl Scout day camps at Spanaway Lake. As a family, we went on Sunday drives in our pink Pontiac station wagon with us kids rocking back and forth in the back seat and singing "She'll Be Comin' around the Mountain" and "Take Me Out to the Ball Game," all the while anticipating the stop for our favorite treat: ice-cream cones. We enjoyed seasonal wiener roasts thanks to Dad's fire pit engineering and Mom's kitchen magic, which produced yummy potato salad and chocolate cake. We went clam digging along Pacific Ocean beaches and camping at Mount Rainier—or Ti'Swaq, as my Native American friends call this mountain standing regal in the Cascade Mountain Range.

Friends liked my parents, who allowed us to have parties in our large living room. Mom served snacks and Dad talked about hunting, fishing, and sports with the guys. Life was orderly and logical, except when Mom was deep in depression, had emotional breakdowns, and went into the hospital for treatment. Life was orderly and logical, except when Dad suddenly stopped "horsing around" with us girls after we reached puberty, flirted with women, and left for weeks at a time to hunt or fish while mom never had a vacation. Growing up, life held an uneven logic with no emotional content.

Logical achieving is cold without emotional being; conversations are empty when they lack emotional color and texture; and soul is missing when there are no eyes to see or ears to hear the sounds of deep, resonant emotion. For twenty-five years, I was lost trying to function without my inner Feminine and its feeling realm.

Hypnotherapy

Talking to Dad as an eight-year-old,
talking to him as an adult,
talking to my eight-year-old,
talking to my adult.
Intense tears
carve an opening deep within.
I buy a teddy bear.

> What irrational laws do we obey, what subjective signals allow us to establish the right direction at any moment, which symbols and myths predominate in a particular conjunction of objects or web of happenings, what meaning can be ascribed to the eye's capacity to pass from visual to visionary power?
>
> —Hayden Herrera, *Frida: A Biography of Frida Kahlo*

CHAPTER 4

BRAINWASHED

Our childhood holds us, shapes us, and teaches us. In later years it is up to us to keep what is true and transmute what is not true.

I was born into a hypnotic spell that held me captive for years. This spell held true for many people worldwide and continues today with a brainwashing that tells females and males that a boyfriend or girlfriend, lover, or spouse will make us happy and whole. I stepped into the spell and acted out the prepared script.

When I was five years old, a neighbor boy and I sneaked our first kiss next to a barn in a nearby field. The kiss made me feel grown up, and keeping it secret made me feel important somehow. Walking to grade school, I kissed another boy along a wooded path. I still remember the scent of pungent green willow, his well-worn leather jacket, quiet manner, and missing fingers on one hand. In sixth grade, I was attracted to the older boys my sister brought home and didn't understand the physical desires that pulled me toward them like a magnet. As a teenager, I was "in love" with my high school sweetheart.

We didn't drink or party. We did wear matching sweaters to school, kiss a lot, explore each other's bodies, and learn the hot pleasures of sex. Like all teenagers, we thought it was a forever kind of love.

My childhood and teenage years revolved around boys and finding love. My sisters and I raced home from school to dance to music televised on *American Bandstand*. I was influenced by songs about teen romance, such as "Puppy Love" by Paul Anka, "Only the Lonely" by Roy Orbison, and "Let It Be Me" by the Everly Brothers, and by drive-in movies' seductive actresses, such as Marilyn Monroe and Elizabeth Taylor. This early stimulation revolved around sexual desire. No one suggested that there was more to life.

Though I planned to go to college and study to be an elementary teacher, teenage hormones and careless choices took me into motherhood at age nineteen. Still a child, I was going to give birth to a child. Shocked and numb, I crawled into bed for several days, hiding under covers, wrestling with two questions that were inextricably linked in that era: *Was I really going to have a child? Did I really want to marry?* Finally, I got out of bed and faced the consequences of my actions. During this time, I didn't talk about the shame I felt, and no one talked to me about their feelings. Later I did hear, from a third party, that one of my sisters was disappointed in me. Once again, feelings went unspoken to rattle around underground—unseen and unheard. In spite of unspoken feelings, family and friends supported us with a lovely bridal shower and church wedding. Can these surface acts of kindness override buried feelings, or do our subconscious and unconscious minds hold unexpressed emotion that requires conscious attention and untangling sooner or later?

I look back at that early time of my life and wonder: where were the parental boundaries that protect a young teenager? The answer I come up with is that since there was no communication about feelings generally, let alone communication about sexual feelings specifically, this silence offered no guidance or direction and led to one choice: let hot hormones dictate. I don't blame my parents. They did their best with the upbringing they experienced and the social patterns they had learned during their lifetimes.

My husband and I moved to Washington State University in Pullman, where he played linebacker on a football scholarship. It was exciting to watch him play in a large stadium and fun to socialize with other players and their wives. We struggled financially, so our entertainment consisted of playing cards or cribbage and dancing at a local tavern to Creedence Clearwater Revival's "Proud Mary." I often strolled my young daughter to campus, visiting Butch the Cougar mascot who was kept in a cage (a custom later identified as "animal cruelty" and discontinued).

Living on Maiden Lane, I remember being pregnant and asking my husband to go for walks. I yearned for something more, something just out of reach. I was looking for the Sacred Feminine through the smell of lilac, green of park, and inner stillness of being. My husband didn't experience this call to nature and introspection. I felt alone. Where was the man to make me happy and whole?

Moving directly from my parents' house with five siblings into another house with a husband didn't allow me time to get to know myself. This missing phase of personal development had an effect on my need for solitude, and my desire to know myself in my inner house. This turning within to listen has been critical in my life. It's how I breathe deeply, sustaining myself inside-out. It's also why I am more comfortable being alone than in social gatherings with surface chitchat.

> Stillness in an empty house
> the rooms all mine to putter about
> I light a candle and listen.

I loved my husband and daughter as much as a teen mother and wife could. I enjoyed cooking, childcare, waitressing, and creating a home on a very small budget—our splurge for the week was root beer floats at the corner A&W. I sewed matching outfits for my daughter and me and made crafts. I still have Christmas banners made of burlap, felt, and assorted trimming that I created back then, when I had more time than money. Yet, lost within, I experienced depression, and, though I now had a man, I was not happy. One winter driving home for Thanksgiving, I looked out the car window at the expanse of dull gray landscape and felt a chill run through my core. I'll never forget that dark void that permeated every cell. They say hell is hot. My experience of hell was cold.

I kept looking for a man (even though I had one) to make me happy and whole. What was this compelling force driving me toward men? Was it genetic information in my DNA to sustain the human species? Was it chemical hormones secreted into bloodstream controlling my physiology and behavior? The "ah-ha" moment came when I sought spiritual answers from books and classes to understand my inner experiences, and learned that I am more than my physical body.

I was elated to discover that a subtle energetic body, the aura, surrounds my physical body and that the aura emanates from all living beings. I realized this subtle body, connecting us energetically, is how I feel kinship with another person, tree, river or even a planet. What a powerful bridge connecting diverse forms of matter! Could the subtle body be the "seat of the soul?"

Within the human aura (etheric body) are chakras that regulate the body's flow of energy (prana). *Chakra* is a Sanskrit term from the sacred language of ancient India. The chakra system, first mentioned in the ancient Vedas, the Hindu books of knowledge, identifies seven chakras known as "wheels of light." These vortexes of energies act as spinning wheels, receiving electromagnetic radiant energy or Light, and downloading this vital life force through the endocrine system and glands that transmit electrochemical impulses throughout the physical body. Each chakra has its own color, location and characteristics. Here is a brief outline:

- First Chakra: The RED root or base chakra represents being grounded in our bodies and the Earth. It is located in the tailbone area at the base of the spine and is associated with the gonads and ovaries in the endocrine system.
- Second Chakra: The ORANGE sacral chakra represents emotions and sexuality. It is located a little below the navel and is associated with the adrenals in the endocrine system.
- Third Chakra: The YELLOW solar plexus chakra represents our power base and the ability to be confident and in control of our lives. It is located just above the navel and is associated with the pancreas in the endocrine system.
- Fourth Chakra: The GREEN heart chakra represents our ability to love unconditionally. It is located near the heart at the center of the chest and is associated with the thymus in the endocrine system.
- Fifth chakra. The BLUE throat chakra represents our ability to communicate through thought and feeling. It is located between the collarbone and larynx on the neck and is associated with the thyroid in the endocrine system.
- Sixth chakra. The INDIGO third-eye chakra represents our ability to see intuitively and psychically. It is located at the center of the forehead and is associated with the pituitary gland in the endocrine system.
- Seventh Chakra: The VIOLET crown chakra represents consciousness as pure awareness, and enlightenment. It is located at the top of the head and is associated with the pineal gland in the endocrine system.

This rainbow spectrum helped me understand the brainwashing spell that shaped me, and so many of my generation, as a young girl and teenager. It revealed, quite vividly, that I was born into an energetic red and orange world where sexuality was the dominant pattern in the collective consciousness. Learning about the chakra system made me realize that red/orange sexual compulsions were the powerful drivers in my life. I was in their grip being carried along with the masses! Could the brainwashing spell be erased? Could a new script be written, a new story told? Yes! This is how I re-write the story:

I use third-eye imaging and see myself born into this world as female and male, with feeling and logic intact. This divine inheritance is a complete package with nothing external to seek. As my spiritual soul descends into this realm of matter and incarnates in human form, I am greeted by a welcoming community. I see boys and men, girls and women, as extensions of my inner male and female. I am lovingly embraced and I lovingly embrace in return, celebrating family and community as parts of myself. I hear drumbeats and chimes, smell sweet lavender, and pungent fir, and see vibrant rainbow colors celebrating S/He, whole and holy.

Body Rainbow

Tingling sensation at the top of head,
airy, spacious feeling at the groin,
currents of energy moving up and down my spine
subtle to dense—dense to subtle.
Spirit and form merging, dancing, creating emotion.
Conscious am I to welcome these currents
knowing them in tone and sound of color.
Conscious am I to sense their lines in my body
connecting me to a larger whole.
Lines drawing pictures
spirit to earth, earth to cosmos,
woman to nature, being to being.
Energy current weaving parts
coloring in the whole.

PATRICIA LEE

Violet moves the spectrum red
green the bridging heart.

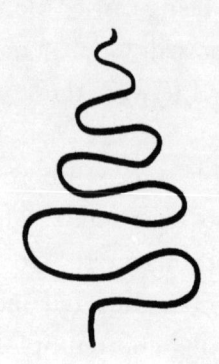

> Every blade of grass has its angel that bends
> over it and whispers, "Grow, grow."
>
> —The Talmud

Chapter 5

Rapture

My life was out of control and I hit bottom. Engulfed in depression and unhealthy behavior I made a choice to change direction. An angel was there to greet me.

Like a puppet on strings, I kept feeling "pulled" to have sexual affairs with men. These strings, colored red/orange and related to sexuality, kept me brainwashed. Though I now knew about lower chakras and their strong influence on me, I had not untangled the strings that held me captive. Inner spiritual work needed to be done before I could move to the next level of awareness and free myself.

This "pull" toward men was not about consciously wanting to have affairs to feed my ego, it was subconscious, as if some force under the surface had me in a chokehold. Though this energetic pattern was not logical, it ruled my life. Were these pulling threads compensating for not being seen or heard as a sensitive child, an effort to get an emotionally unavailable "daddy" to love me, or reaction to Mom's depression and silent world? Why was I in this chokehold anyway, and how could I break free?

When I did have an affair, there were no lights blazing, no bells ringing, and I was left empty again. I had thought another man would make me feel alive and complete. But no, I felt even more alone. Did that experience change me? No. Unconscious of anything higher than my lowest chakras, these energetic vibrations were in control. Certainly, there is nothing wrong with earthy red/orange chakra energies when they are part of one whole system of expression, but when they are separated from the whole and stuck in overdrive, the result is unstable behavior. It's similar to an eight-cylinder vehicle running on two cylinders—limited in power and performance.

Occasionally, my husband and I experimented socially with drugs. One night, we drove to a concert in Seattle with friends. I was high, out of my body, stretching elastic-like above the cityscape. Colored kaleidoscopic patterns faded in and out, bringing more paranoia than pleasure. The next morning, my husband and friends had come down from their drugged haze, but I was still "spaced out." I sat in my living room dazed, staring out the window like a zombie. Senses were cut off, no longer feeding data of perception to my brain-body. Was I ever going to feel normal again? Then an observing voice said, "This is what it's like being in a mental institution." I heard the message loud and clear. Right then and there I made a pact with heaven that if my senses returned to body, I would not take drugs again. Hours later, much to my relief, my senses returned.

That scare was the day I turned my life around! Feeling like a bird let out of a cage, I started jogging on country roads where I lived. I was now choosing an upward path, ready to escape pulls toward men, drugs, and depression. I felt alone in the world because everything looked different now; I was different. Music helped me cope. Cat Stevens' song "Peace Train" gave me a sense of hope, and the flute melody of Moody Blues' "Voices in the Sky" lifted my spirits. I became a happier woman and mother—one who had made a new choice. I remember taking my young daughter on walks along our country roads, breathing the fresh air and cheerfully chatting with horses in the field. When we passed the mailbox of "Mr. and Mrs. Pickle," we laughed and laughed. These sweet little moments in life gave me a new sense of well-being.

Elizabeth, the hostess at the Tacoma restaurant where I worked as a waitress, taught metaphysics, a philosophy from Ancient Greece that refers to an idea, doctrine, or reality outside the five physical senses and material reality. I accepted her invitation to attend a class. Through her, I learned about astral travel, meditation, auras, extrasensory perception, karma, and experienced séances, visualization, and psychometry (where one holds a physical object and psychically "reads" its story). For example, I held a woman's ring and saw her singing onstage in a blue dress. Though these concepts were new to me, I was receptive and digested them easily.

During my first meditation in the bedroom of our little house in Parkland, I felt a charged energetic presence enter from the east window and move toward me. In a state of tranquil receptivity, my nerves held steady as I saw a band of white feathers and heard the name "Michael." An otherworldly substance enveloped me in a cloud of glory. I continued to hold steady. The etheric energetic presence then dissipated to nothingness, similar to turning the radio dial on, to high volume, and then turning it low and off. This miraculous heavenly visitation caused no paranoia nor did it cut off my senses like the artificial, drug-induced high. In fact, this "natural" high gave me an expanded sense of myself. Lifted into a state of peace I wore a robe of tranquility for days. My reality had shifted and I felt it in my flesh, blood and bones!

When I share my experience of this angel visitation with people, most of them receive it with a blank look in their eyes and a flat tone in their voice. Do they doubt my experience or do they not believe in angels? Or are they afraid of the unknown and their own inner feminine language and terrain?

> Within a Light, hidden in fog,
> destined winds rolled the fog away
> and I was found in Light's ray.
> Why me? Why now? Where will it lead?
> First steps taken guided by Light,
> new meaning on all it shines.
> No hiding, no ignoring
> will dim Light's ray.
> Light is forever to stay.

Anxiously, I asked my teacher about the meditation with white feathers and energetic being. Her response was "Oh, that's Archangel Michael. He is visiting a lot of people on the planet these days." That explained it! The band of feathers was a wing—a perfect Angel introduction! This otherworldly encounter may not have been a big deal to my teacher, but it was a big deal to me. It changed my perception of reality assuring me that I was not alone. Suddenly, I no longer feared death. Being introduced to Archangel Michael and his enveloping rays of Light ignited my passionate creativity. I started to write profusely in response to the feelings and thoughts pouring through me. My inner feminine had found an outlet for her long-silent voice. She was in rapture.

> Up, up, and away,
> leaving earth
> with petty problems behind.
> Up, up, and away,
> where sweet music greets you,
> loving souls meet you,
> and peace is all around.

My rapture experience was very spiritual and even religious. I wrote this poem in 1974 to reflect my new passion and the push back I was receiving from some people around me. How could I change so quickly? How could I leave earthly dramas behind and choose to attend church?

How could I turn my back on the life I knew? I could because I was touched by the Light of an angel.

Rapture

I walk in thy way, O Lord,
though others may condemn,
I walk in thy way.
Thy current is my inspiration,
thy Light is my Light,
thy strength is my strength.
Without thee I am nothing.
Others know not me,
yet I know me.
Others know not thee,
yet it matters not
for I know thee.
I rest in thee
letting thy radiance by my radiance,
thy vibrancy be my vibrancy,
thy spontaneity be my spontaneity.
Nothing can turn me from thee.
Thou art my peace, my joy,
thou art my purpose on earth.
Let come what may
I walk in thy way.

> The only myth that is going to be worth thinking
> about in the immediate future is one that is talking
> about the planet… and everybody on it.
>
> —Joseph Campbell, *The Power of Myth*

Chapter 6

Her Story ~ Herstory

Lifted to a state of rapture, my reality changed. How would I contribute and share my rapture with the world?

My metaphysics teacher claimed to be spiritual, yet she didn't always treat people kindly. I thought this odd. It was my first insight into "spiritual" people not walking their talk. I thanked her, nonetheless, for all that she had contributed to my awareness, and soon moved on.

I followed my heart and learned from teachings of Eckankar, Charles and Myrtle Fillmore, Edgar Cayce, Brugh Joy, and yoga. I rebelled when it came to yoga. When told to hold my thumb and finger in a specific position, or mudra, I thought it excluded those who didn't have a thumb, finger, or hand. This rebellious streak followed me throughout my life. My authority was within, and I didn't want to follow outer rules or structures. I kept moving, knowing I belonged somewhere, knowing there was a path for me. When in doubt, the answer always came:

> You are on your path here/now,
> learning your lessons here/now,

giving your love here/now.

Unity Church is a healing ministry based on the power of prayer and positive thinking, teaching that God lives within each person, and interpreting the Bible metaphysically. I taught Sunday school with my children beside me and felt at home. At Unity, I met a group of people who were reading and discussing *Jonathan Livingston Seagull* by Richard Bach. This book spoke to my inner child and my soul. I was captivated by Jonathan's freedom of flight which gave me a sense of my own spiritual wings. Others must have had a similar soul connection with the book. It was on the *New York Times* Best Seller list for thirty-eight weeks in 1972 and topped the *Publishers Weekly* list of bestselling novels in the United States in 1972 and 1973. I related to Jonathan Livingston Seagull, who felt out of place with his flock that spent their day squabbling over food. He said, "You've got to understand that a seagull is an unlimited idea of freedom, an image of the Great Gull, and your whole body, from wingtip to wingtip, is nothing more than thought itself." I, like Jonathan, wanted to fly higher within myself and with others.

Twenty years later, my spiritual wings landed me in a local peace and justice organization called Sixth Sense, where I volunteered my time as Volunteer Coordinator. We occasionally received phone calls from people asking for a psychic reading. No, we were not that kind of sixth sense! We represented the Sixth Congressional District and were "making sense" to stop the production of nuclear weapons, and were putting pressure on local politicians. These calls gave the staff a chuckle. My interest focused on inner peace and on meditation that transcended boundaries and borders. I valued local citizen exchange projects with the Soviet Union and meeting with members of local churches involved in social and environmental justice. I organized volunteers for mailing parties, phone banks, and peace marches and wrote the following article for our Earth Day newsletter in 1992. The words ring true today, these many years later.

Earth Day is a time when people around the world think about and act upon the choices that must be made to protect the future of our planet. It's a good time to consider the global myth which Joseph Campbell refers to in his book *The Power of Myth*, (Doubleday/1988).

> "Myths are stories of our search through the ages for truth, for meaning, for significance. We all need to tell our story and to understand our story… the only myth that is going to be worth thinking about in the immediate future is one that is talking about the planet… and everybody on it."

Who are the authors of such a myth? We are—we the people of grassroots, we the people who care about our social, economic, political, environmental, agricultural, and educational values and systems. And how do we write the myth? We write it by getting in touch with inner values. Getting in touch with my inner values, I'd like to contribute to the global myth.

Equal Rights for Mother Earth

Mother Earth has a right to clean and free-flowing waters.

She has a right to an aura, an atmosphere that is pure.

She has a right to breathe deeply through pores of open and green space.

She has a right to healthy soil from which to feed her plants, animals, and peoples.

She has a right to natural beauty of wetlands, forests, mountains, and oceans.

She has a right for her people to have wilderness in which to be still and reflect.

She has a right to a balanced population sustaining dynamic equilibrium.

She has a right that all life forms contribute to the vibrant ecosystem of life.

What is your contribution—your page—in the myth being created? It is a page that only you can write. Write it. Share it. Be it.

Volunteer management experience at Sixth Sense opened the door at Children's Home Society of Washington (CHSW), where I was employed for eighteen years as volunteer and special events coordinator, public speaker, and fundraiser. Giving public talks I was occasionally asked by someone in the audience where I worked before CHSW. I would tell the story of Sixth Sense and how I got tired of angry people working for peace. Responses ranged from laughter to silence, telling me a lot about the mind-set of the audience. I never discussed my inner spiritual journey with family, friends, or colleagues. I did journal, sketch, and blog about the language of the Sacred Feminine, as it shaped me moment-by-moment, day-by-day.

I became a member of John Denver's Windstar Foundation and participated in a local chapter. One Earth Day, we sponsored a poetry-reading event at the Antique Sandwich Company, owned by a family of peace and social-justice advocates. I wrote and recited *Her Story/Herstory*, the poem below. We published a booklet that featured our community expression of art, poetry, and stories. This experience of grassroots synergy was a new high for me and now I had a grounded voice of the Sacred Feminine: Mother Earth.

Her Story / Herstory

Mother Earth turns… a day begins.

Mother Earth cries… a flood moves.

Mother Earth shrugs… a valley is carved.

Mother Earth fumes… a mountain rises.

Mother Earth shifts… a season awakes.

Mother Earth blinks… a civilization is gone.

Mother Earth flies… an orbit is patterned.

Mother Earth spins… a galaxy dances.

Mother Earth loves… a life is born.

Mother Earth turns… a day is done.

Magic is the bloodstream of the universe.

—*Willow*, the movie

Chapter 7
Pagan God Pan

I followed my heart, letting it guide me moment by moment through daily life, watching and listening for signs. If something felt right I went that direction. I was on a mystical path and the "yellow brick road" was opening before me.

A charismatic husband and wife team spoke at Unity Church, introducing the Emissaries of Divine Light (EDL), a global spiritual network founded in 1932 by Lloyd Meeker. These two captivated me, sharing the EDL mission, which was "to assist in the spiritual generation of humanity under the inspiration of the spirit of God," teaching that human beings are "divine by nature and that our divinity is experienced as it is expressed in service to the world."

> *All people have the opportunity to deepen their attunement with the universal wisdom and love within them. That connection allows us to know ourselves more fully and to express who we are in the world. The future of our planet depends on this for humanity as a whole. …The mission of Emissaries of Divine Light is the spiritual regeneration of humanity,"*
> —www.emissaries.org/about-us/

This correlation of self-healing and planetary healing resonated with me and took deeper root in my life.

I attended classes at 100 Mile House in British Columbia and Sunrise Ranch in Loveland, Colorado, both thriving communities with large organic gardens, communal kitchens and dining rooms, residential housing, offices, and classrooms. As a shy newbie, I was in awe of seasoned Emissaries who fit in and knew the day-to-day routines. I harvested garden vegetables and prepared them in the large kitchen beside men and women from all over the world. One afternoon, I cleaned vegetables in freezing water and my hands wanted to revolt. Was this a test to see how long one could tolerate discomfort? It was a good lesson in mind over matter and staying centered.

Evening services, held twice a week, were especially reverent, with candles, flowers, music, and silence. Emissary centers attracted talented musicians, dancers, healers, artists, poets, speakers, cooks, and gardeners. I was a quiet participant, thriving on spiritual teachings.

EDL services, based on the original teachings of Lloyd Meeker, were offered by co-founder Lord Martin Cecil. These writings were distributed to centers around the world where local EDL "focalizers," (male "points of focus") read them. I attended Sunday service at the center in Seattle with warm respect for those participating. EDL felt like family to me…a spiritual family that gave me a new sense of belonging now that so much had changed in my personal life. After service, a comment period provided opportunity to respond spontaneously, from the heart. This flowing spiritual expression (without analyses) reminded me of grade school's double-dutch jump roping and knowing when to jump in at just the right moment. The art of responding was to wrap around or sense the spiritual substance that the service engendered and then to communicate logically so that one's words added meaning to the collective experience. Though I didn't know it at the time, this taught me to integrate intuitive knowing (feminine) and sequential logic (masculine) through the spoken word. My inner Sacred Feminine and Sacred Masculine were relating before I became conscious of their presence.

"Attunements" were "energy medicine," as male and female practitioners placed hands above the different endocrine glands of the client. These glands were considered contact points that served as portals for universal life energy to move through the physical body. The "radiation" of attunements gave me an overall feeling of peace, relaxation, and lightness. The subtle yet vibrant energy currents moving around and through my body gave me the sense that I was plugging in to a divine life force. Attunement also referred to a personal practice in the conscious evolution of humanity. Attunement became my inner quest, as did the mantra, "Let love radiate without concern for results."

This path was not one that my husband chose to follow. I left books I was reading around the house, to see if they would catch his eye—books on personal growth and consciousness, such as *Be Here Now* by Ram Dass and *Keys to Higher Consciousness* by Ken Keyes. He did read a couple of them but did not have the hunger I did. Our diverse appetites led to a separation and divorce.

> Thank you for friendship,
> all the caring you do.
> Thank you for fathering
> our children, too.
> Thank you for letting
> life give what it will.
> Thank you for space
> that love does fill.

After several years in the Emissaries of Divine Light, moving from one spiritual community to another, listening and responding to male focalizers, I hit a ceiling. I was ready for something more. Nature, wilderness, and Goddess called, shape-shifting "church" into a loose and earthy experience. A new aspect of my Sacred Feminine was coming alive, and she wanted more room to breathe, stretch, and move.

> In the hush
> amidst the noise of humankind crying
> and Mother Earth dying,
> Goddess is born.
> Initiated at hand of divinity
> on wings of ascending current
> to be given and received as bride.
> Goddess of love, circulate thy essence.
> Goddess of fertility, cultivate thy currents.
> Nurture green again upon land
> of heart, mind, and body.

I joined the Blue Moon Medicine Lodge under the teachings of Grandmother Berniece Falling Leaves. Men and women gathered in circle to drum, chant, and do ceremony, as well as learn dream interpretation, hand analysis, and polarity therapy. I was gifted a large turtle shell from a circle sister and found a stick with one end that looked like a turtle's head. It fit into the shell perfectly. I attached beads inside the shell to make my turtle medicine rattle. On a spirit quest to *She Who Watches*, a famous Native American petroglyph (carved into the rock) and pictograph (drawn or painted onto rock) in the Columbia River Gorge, I received my medicine blanket. Grandmother gave me a spirit name: "Yellow Turtle Spirit." And months later, I heard from within, "Laughing Waters." So putting them together, my spirit name became "Yellow Turtle Spirit in Laughing Waters."

Church was now transformed. Instead of sitting on chairs within walls while listening to a male speak of God, I was now in circle, rattling and attuning to spirit, nature, and Goddess. I too was transformed. And then, one morning, I met Pagan God Pan.

S/He Dragon

On ley line of earth
turning to greet sun
co-creating dawn of new day,
on ley line of still space
between worlds of night and day,
a hearty presence laughs in my ear
of merry-making and joy,
very signal that cues bird song.
I came to know him that day
as Pan, horned pagan god.
He is of the rocks that spoke to me saying,
"Take me home to your windowsill."
He is of the seals that surfaced
for the four of us sitting circle, coven style,
adding magic to the mystical day.
He is of the tree that caught my eye
in northern country,
Cedrus deodara of draping green,
feminine gown of grace.
He dances and plays at home in misty rain,
singing to mortals, "Undress, and be free."
His presence, his tune
arouse erotic energies of subtle nature.
As I listen, he guides me to faery country
where sexuality of earth body dances new song.

Trees are poems that the earth writes upon the sky.

—Kahlil Gibran, *Sand and Foam*

Chapter 8

Ever Green ~ A Story

Goddess came to life as a living presence. I wrote this story to capture our fertile relationship.

Goddess reveals herself when busyness ceases. I used to work two jobs; now I work one. I used to attend many meetings; now I attend none. I used to live in an apartment with pavement and noise; now I live in a little house with green grass and trees. I used to be too busy to tend a garden; now friends and I prepare a backyard plot for sowing of seed. This new stillness in my life has a way of bending time—so much so that time stands still—allowing me to be present in the moment.

Goddess reveals moon mysteries of my sexual nature. Ovulation, a full-moon phase with gravitational pull at its peak, is potent as ovaries ride fertility waves, releasing eggs during my menstrual cycle. Feeling aggressive sexually, I want to grab the closest man. I have learned to manage these chemical urges, knowing that I'm more than red/orange chemistry and expression.

There's an evergreen tree near my house, a focus during my moon cycle. I am drawn to this tree and its circulating vitality that receives nourishment from above, pulls sap up from roots, and pushes it outward through branching arms and leafing fingers. Connected energetically, tree and I share one common electromagnetic current with positive and negative charges running from crown to root and root to crown.

During ovulation, my skin hungers to touch and to be touched. How natural, then, to relate to trees—the skin of the earth. Trees and skin absorb and transmit light energy to maintain healthy equilibrium. Trees protect Mother Earth; skin protects my earth. Trees and skin are communicators of love.

I watch the city of Tacoma cut down tree after tree, making way for concrete buildings and asphalt roads, all in the name of development and "progress." I watch living green decrease and barren gray increase. Where are the sacred groves of old? Where can lovers go to honor magnetic tides of fertility in rhythm with Goddess? Trees, the cells of Earth Mother's body, die just as cells of human bodies die. Disease, both personal and planetary, are signs of a barren world hungering for love's fertility.

I think about getting politically active, approaching city planning in defense of green and tree. For now, it's enough being still, engaged in a charged relationship with tree that is both uplifting and grounding. Relationship that is kinship with life—evergreen.

> One does not become enlightened by imagining figures of light,
> but by making the darkness conscious. The latter procedure,
> however, is disagreeable and therefore not popular.
>
> —C. G. Jung

CHAPTER 9
EMOTIONAL WHEEL

Emotions controlled me until I experienced myself as more than my emotions. In detached observation I looked back on my life and its early influences, and I looked within at the emotional wheel turning and re-turning.

Growing up next door to a country store with assorted penny candy initiated my love for sweets. Back in those days, candy was displayed in a wooden framed glass case at the front of the store and one could choose from licorice, Tootsie Pops, waxed figures with juice, taffy, gummy bears, coconut fruits, and, my favorite, molasses Mary Janes. These treats in little brown paper bags accompanied me as I walked to and from grade school. They gave me a sense of comfort.

Mom was an excellent cook. I enjoyed her homemade chicken potpies, bread and gravy, sourdough pancakes, and comforting casseroles. Actually, there wasn't anything Mom made that I didn't enjoy. As "Fatty Patty" in third grade, it was obvious that I loved food.

Pronouncing the letter *r* in grade school was difficult and I was excused from class to spend time with a speech therapist who taught me fire-truck siren sounds of *r-r-r-r*. One day at the candy store, I asked for "wum life savas." The owner criticized my speech and I ran home crying. Another emotional upset came when my sister, who is two years older, had a group of boys at the house. I was so shy that I ran past them up the stairs, hoping they wouldn't see me. Of course, they did and proceeded to laugh. And if my shyness wasn't bad enough, I turned red with embarrassment in so many situations. Did those in my presence notice? You bet they did, and I will never understand why they always had to say, "Look, she's turning red." Those humiliating moments in childhood are tame compared to what many other children endure. Yet they were character-building opportunities that shaped my sense of self. And what did that shaping look like? Did I take on a victim role to blame others, did I become helpless and, to compensate, act out aggressively; did I repress the hurts and experience them later as depression and mood swings, or did I transform my own hurt and heal myself? Thanks to spiritual support, inside and out, I eventually did the latter.

Mom experienced severe depression. She never talked about it; no one talked about it. Instead, she shut herself off and hid behind bedroom doors and bathroom walls. Yet, her emotions could not be hidden and had their own voice that grew to a crescendo, sending Mom to the hospital with a nervous breakdown. I remember days she wouldn't speak, instead sitting stone-faced for hours at the kitchen table, and days she would be rude to people on the home business phone. As a young child, I felt sad for Mom in the privacy of our home, and I felt embarrassed for her in the ears of the public. My feelings went unspoken, buried under the surface of consciousness to rattle around without any order or placement.

As a young girl, starting at age eight, I experienced my own "behind the walls" bouts with depression. I never lashed out at others. I took the dark times out on myself, hitting bathroom walls with my fists, choking down sobs so I couldn't be heard, and feeling so miserable that I thought I wanted to die.

As a teenager, I was very moody and remember having arguments with my high school sweetheart and running away. In the middle of a city, I jumped out of the car and ran. I had no experience communicating feelings within my family and thus no experience communicating feelings with him. In fact, I never learned to communicate my feelings to myself! How could I? I didn't know that inner emotion and logic existed. My fight response erupted in the bathroom and my flight response flared up with my boyfriend. These emotional reactions lacked boundaries, as I had no way to determine when feelings ended and logic began. These threads of my psyche entangled in a distorted web that would reveal itself later in life in the form of codependent relationships and compulsive eating patterns.

Mood swings and depression eased up when I "saw the Light" at age twenty-five and learned I was more than my feelings, thoughts, and actions. My ego could now step aside. And as a spiritual being of Light expressing through matter in human form, I could observe myself from a place of nonattachment. From this observation point, I watched positive and negative emotions dance in dynamic tension. This energy-in-motion (e-motion) created an upward spiral of evol/change, different from the downward spiral of evil/stagnation. What makes the difference? In my experience, the answer is simple: Light! Light that energizes everything it touches.

Letting emotional energy move moment-by-moment, day-by-day is critical to self-awareness and healing. I know this spiral dance. It moves circularly like the medicine wheel and begins in the east.

>
> Artistic brushstroke
> pulling, pushing e-motion
> like a wheel cultivating, turning
> the soil of my being.
> A massage of the soul
> moving me toward wholeness,
> toward Light.

Gaia turns to greet the morning sun and Her life forms stir, awakening in response. The wheel of life begins in the east with potential for ascension, growth, and unfoldment. It's a seed rising out of the ground, a baby born, a new job or relationship. East is the dawn of a new day and cycle.

From east, I turn south, knowing bright and happy energy-in-motion (e-motion) as I grow in potential. What makes you bright and happy? For me it's being active, outgoing and positive—from within—so the activity can be inside (writing and cooking) or outside (gardening and hiking). I know sooner or later this e-motion will shift. How do I know? Because someone told me, or I read it in a book? No. I know because I have been around this e-motional wheel again and again.

South shifts, moving me west, where more alchemical change takes place. Here brightness decreases and temperatures drop, in synch with setting sun. I turn inward, aware of the circular motion of the e-motional wheel.

From west, e-motion moves me north where I turn cold, dark, and void. Years ago, I would stay frozen in the north for days in what felt like a depressed cave of gravity. There were days that I could not get out of bed or leave the house. This was uncomfortable, yet I reminded myself it would soon be sunny again. That didn't diminish the intensity, however. My ongoing mantra was "The higher I fly, the lower I dive." Now, many years later, the circular wheel turns more smoothly, e-motion more fluid, and I don't experience dark depression the same way,

From the north, with an expanded view of the horizon, I am released into the east to dance another e-motional and alchemical cycle. Here, new potential for ascension, growth, and unfoldment awaits the transmutation of Light.

I saw the angel in the marble and carved until I set him free.

—Michelangelo

Chapter 10

Wearing Grief ~ A Teaching

I attended a lecture about wilderness awareness and noticed that the person who greeted me was cold and distant and that some others in attendance would not make eye contact. I wondered what was behind this unfriendly body language. I wanted open-hearted connection but soon discovered this was not going to happen. Why did people wrap themselves in unhappiness? Were they in grief? What would it take for them to wear a different garment?

Grief is typically known as emotional loss (past or present) that triggers expressions of anger, stress, unhappiness, sorrow, and misery. One can feel loss when a person or pet dies, or a relationship ends. Losing a personal relationship is losing a part of oneself. It has an immediate effect on your life and shakes you to the core. Another type of loss is relationship with oneself. This occurs when there is a lack of positive feedback in one's environment—a lack of not being seen and heard. This can happen in childhood, as a teenager or an adult. This neglect can create myriad patterns of grief from over-eating to over-achieving. Besides personal grief there is collective grief associated with Mother Earth. Her loss of cultures and peoples throughout history is our loss.

This collective grief is also felt as we witness the ongoing destruction of forests, rivers and oceans, and soil.

Grief has physical, cognitive, behavioral, social, and spiritual dimensions and can be expressed in ways that are sub-conscious and unconscious. Are you consciously aware of grief and how it shows up in your life through your day-to-day living expression?

Do you wear grief as an undergarment so no one can see? Or do you wear it loudly on your sleeve? Perhaps you're not even aware of grief. Well, let me ask you a few questions so you can determine for yourself if grief is a garment in your daily wardrobe.

Let's start by asking your feet, "Do you wear grief?"

Do your feet dance through the day, or are they heavy and weighed down by cares known and unknown? Do they take you places you'd rather not be, *with people you*'d rather not be with? Do your feet support you, grounded in a dance of well-being?

Let's ask your hands, "Do you wear grief?"

Do your hands reach out to others, or are they hiding in the shadows? Do they extend a rainbow of emotions? Do they dance in dishwater *and stay calm in rush*-hour commute? Are your hands in tune with dancing feet?

Let's ask your mouth, "Do you wear grief?"

Does your mouth express tones that create connection with others? Does it smile and laugh with splashes of joy, or is it sad and gloomy? Does your mouth smile sweet purity, or is it spewing bitter toxins into the atmosphere? Is your mouth resounding the beat of dancing feet and hands?

Let's ask your eyes, "Do you wear grief?"

Do your eyes see the world through a lens reflecting shadow or light? Do you see through muddy waters, or is your aura clear? Do you see sparkle in others' eyes and rays of hope in momentary opportunities? Do your eyes celebrate the dance of life around you?

Let's ask your ears, "Do you wear grief?"

Do your ears hear only the negativity that is so prominent in this world? Or are they attuned to a beat that uplifts to another reality? Do your ears echo despair, or do they accompany dancing eyes? Do your ears hear the music of the spheres in the city, in the forest, in a crowd of strangers, and alone?

Let's ask your nose, "Do you wear grief?"

Does your nose pick up scents that are carried in the moment? Does it notice subtle changes in the wind? Does your nose inhale deeply, nourishing your cells? Or is it plugged up and closed off? Does your nose participate in the dance of feet, hands, mouth, eyes, and ears?

Let's ask your skin and body, "Do you wear grief?"

Does your skin hide, ashamed of its shape, age, or size? Is it lethargic due to the barrage of criticism it has received? Does your skin shrivel in fear when life knocks at its door? Or does it extend a welcome mat and let joy dance through?

How did you answer those questions? Did they allow you to take a look at grief in your body and in your life? The body's emotional expressions cannot be hidden and tell the world what you are experiencing and how you are feeling. Are you now considering that grief may be part of your everyday wardrobe?

There are many books on the subject of healing ourselves with prayer, meditation, yoga, visualization, affirmation, hypnosis, and shamanic journeying. The good news is that your body is intelligent in its process of healing. It will guide you when you are tired of chaos, when you have reached a breaking point, and when you are ready. It will guide you into and through core issues layer by layer.

The process does get hot. It does get intense. At one time, the experience felt like I was being ripped out at the core, and in this healing intensity, two words bubbled up from my deep unconscious: "Sun dance." With the ripping, came new "tissue" that felt protective—yes, like a garment. Some people travel hundreds and thousands of miles to attend this Native American ceremony. Emotional grief brought the Sun dance to me.

Healing grief is not a one-time process. It is part of living in this realm of dark and light duality by giving us ongoing opportunity to transmute patterns of grief into golden rays of emotional expression. Core grief paves the way to core healing. I encourage you to go there, recognize the garments that keep you bound, and then name and release them. Your feet, hands, mouth, eyes, ears, nose, skin, and whole body will thank you.

Transmute your grief, and wear a wardrobe of shining joy!

> As all matter is ergoconscious and responsive to formative pressures from above, there must be in our terrestrial context as well as in ourselves, centres and channels through which cosmic energies pass and in which they blend.
>
> —Mary Scott, *Kundalini in the Physical World*

Chapter 11

Kundalini Dragon

My body and life were forever changed by a sudden strike of Kundalini fire. Thrown into a paralyzed state, with my future at risk, I, once again, held steady in Light.

The 8th International Human Unity Conference (HUC), held at the University of British Columbia in 1981, changed my life. I heard Marilyn Ferguson, author of *The Aquarian Conspiracy: Personal and Social Transformation in the 1980s*, (J. P. Tarcher, Inc./Los Angeles/ 1980), speak about the paradigm shift, the holographic universe, intuition as natural knowledge, mystical unity of humankind, and planetary consciousness. Marilyn Ferguson summed up the conspiracy as "both enlightenment and mystery… power and humility… interdependence and individuality."

The Aquarian Conspiracy's description of "whole brain knowing" gave me insight into how my brain functions. I didn't process information in the usual linear, detailed way, tracing ideas and thoughts from point A to point B. My process was nonlinear and holistic, going from A to Z all at once. It was intuitive, an instantaneous knowing. I was glad to have these puzzle pieces identified so I could fit them together and better understand myself. According to Marilyn Ferguson, "There is a tendency to think of intuition as separate from the intellect. More accurately, intuition might be said to encompass intellect." Listening to Marilyn speak, a sense of relief welled up in me as her words mirrored my own intuitive nature.

Presenters at the conference shared my values and spoke my language, giving me a sense of homecoming. They included Barbara Marx Hubbard with Conscious Evolution, Gerald Jampolsky and Diane Cerincione with Attitudinal Healing, and John Graham with The Giraffe Project. The audience was educated and in "new age" transformation, inspired by personal stories, and invited to sing along to upbeat music. Voices and spirits bonded, lifting us as one collective body.

We talked and sang about transformation, and we experienced it. I felt like a cheerleader again jumping up and down in my conference seat while cheering for my new transformation team! I was hooked on this natural and synergetic high, eager to attend the next HUC in Oxford, England, with friends from my church, the Emissaries of Divine Light.

A couple of weeks before my departure, I experienced dizzy spells. This was not a chronic condition, so when they subsided, I knew I would be able to travel to England.

At the conference, I registered, located my room, and enjoyed lunch with new friends—all of us bursting with enthusiasm. What did I have for lunch on my first visit to England? Mom, being detail-oriented, would have made note of this in her diary. I did not.

Walking back to my room, I felt a sudden snap at the back of my neck and my legs collapsed. My world was instantly pulled out from under me. A man from South Africa assisted me to my room and stayed with me to make sure I was okay. I soon discovered I was not okay. I could not walk! Somehow, I had lost my brain-spine-feet connection. This man offered massage, and physical touch did help me feel more connected to my body, but I was going nowhere. For three days, I was alone in that room. The only time I got out of bed was when I crawled to the bathroom—I could not stand upright.

I did not want a Western medical doctor to treat me, nor did I want to go to a hospital. Western medicine doesn't acknowledge energy fields, chakras, or spiritual Light as part of one's physiological health and well-being. I knew this was not an ordinary condition, so I turned within, listened, and watched for guidance. I also knew that Archangel Michael was with me and did the only thing that I could, focusing on a speck of white light at my forehead, my third-eye chakra.

At first, the speck was so very tiny, but it held the hope of a mustard seed. Was I scared? Yes! Did I wonder if I would walk again? Yes! If this was a test, I was a good student. I kept third-eye focus moment-by-moment, hour-by-hour, and day-by-day for three days. In a frozen state, I held steady in Light and Light increased. Is there an English legend about a lady frozen in a lake? I sensed I was this lady as I watched underwater images come and go.

By the third day, I started to feel some stability at my core and was able to stand upright and walk. I attended a couple of conference sessions but noticed I was not mentally grounded in my body, as if my brain and body were disconnected. Though I could walk again I had another test in front of me: fly out of England and return to Washington State. Floating in brain-body fog made this extremely difficult.

Boarding the plane in England and arriving in Canada was a relief. My body parts were stable enough to get me this far. The next challenge was driving home. How could I make intelligent choices and coordinated movements with my head in the clouds and my body somewhere in the distant mist? In this state of suspension time seemed to stand still.

"Will I ever get home?" I wondered. "Will I ever feel grounded again?" I asked the universe. Once again I held the hope of a mustard seed and moment by moment, traffic sign by traffic sign, turn by turn, I arrived home. Years later, I read that a sudden activation of Kundalini in one's spine and nervous system can kill a person. Though I lived through it my brain was changed forever.

Light saved me from drugs, depression, and affairs with men; now it saved me from Kundalini serpentine fire. Light became my "Savior." This early experience on my spiritual path is why I use white Light to encircle myself, family, loved ones, unknown ones, my car, my home, and Gaia. If Light could protect and heal my physical body, it could do the same for other bodies.

In the book *When the Drummers Were Women,* (ThreeRiversPress/1997), Layne Redmond writes, "The energy of the Goddess—the Kundalini—sleeps coiled, snakelike, at the base of the spine." In *Spiritual Sex,* (PocketBooks/1997), Nik Douglas writes, "Kundalini… is a female power, a Goddess, unfathomable, creative and inherently spiritual… the raw, untamed sexual-energy Goddess." Kundalini had struck me at the back of the neck with a swift force that took me out of my ordinary brain-body and into a different brainwave frequency and dimension.

After this mind-body altering experience, taking care of my young children, as well as engaging socially with adults, was difficult. Feeling displaced, I could not explain my situation to anyone, because I didn't understand it. My children eventually lived with their father while I lived close by, searching for my lost soul and missing body parts.

Later in life, I felt deep grief about the loss of connection with my children during their young lives. It saddened me that I was not fully present in mind and body to nurture them, watch them grow, and participate in many of their day-to-day activities. I feel that I sacrificed time with my young children to follow the path of the Sacred Feminine.

I came to understand and accept this as neither good nor bad but as the way our lives unfolded. While I dearly loved my children, I had to learn to love myself.

Some sources say that before we are born into this realm, we choose our circumstances in order to learn lessons in this school of life, Planet Earth. I like this way of looking at one's life, and how it underscores personal responsibility. No one else is to blame. My mantra, at that early time on my spiritual path, was "Let love radiate without concern for results." That love had to do with finding my missing parts in order to love myself, an essential foundation before one can love others. Now to assist my spiritual evolution was a fiery relationship with Kundalini that would evolve in its own mystical way. My responsibility was to be conscious of its presence and learn from its ancient, mystical wisdom.

Itzhak Bentova, a Czech-born Israeli scientist, inventor, mystic and author, and early pioneer of consciousness studies, said that consciousness is "the capacity of a system to respond to stimuli." The following dream and visions were just that stimuli to spark, within me, a new wave of consciousness.

> Dream, 2/1993
> A creature, spiral in design, emerges from a dark mist. I pick it up and peel something away. Salamander has come to me! Tenderly protecting it with my hands, I look for a place to set it free near the forest for protection and water for nourishment.

Dreamtime salamander had an emotional impact on me that emanated from my heart and solar plexus chakras. It was an arcing energy—circular and motherly as I birthed a new part of myself. Salamander was so dear to me that I hired a local artist to draw a logo of it for my business cards and website, Community Threads.

Vision, 4/1993

Strange energies present this day. I am irritable and withdrawn. I see salamander mouth above me, larger than me. I see rough, scaly flesh and wings. I think, *Flying... and... dragon*! Is my salamander turning into a dragon? He's much bigger now.

Vision, 7/1993

I look down the neck of a dragon, seeing above his eyes. I see what he sees. I am inside dragon, looking directly through his eyes. I have felt motherly toward salamander and dragon—as if they were something external to nurture. This new sensation of wrapping around something inside me is a feeling of integration from within—I am dragon!

Author Mary Scott writes in *Kundalini in the Physical World*, (PenquinGroup/1983), "All energies at work in bodies become Kundalini forces as soon as they enter dense matter. Similarly all becomes part of the earth as soon as it manifests within its field of forces."

My dense matter had been the recipient of Kundalini and this "field of forces" had much more to reveal.

Relationship is but one way in which we experience ourselves.

—Arnold Mindell, *The Dreambody in Relationships*

Chapter 12

Fertility

I was single for many years after my husband and I divorced. He and I remained friends to model for our three children that a relationship may change form, but friendship is constant if people choose.

The next man in my life taught me about childhood wounds, women who love too much, codependence, and sexual addiction. He also taught me to golf, invited me to travel the world and to dine in fine restaurants. Our relationship held drama and dysfunction that revolved around my insecurity and his lusting after other women. I spoke with him about his womanizing and he insisted I was hallucinating. I felt hurt being with a man who "loves" me and then witnessing him project sexual energy toward other women. This crazy-making didn't cause me to end the relationship. I was stuck in the drama, playing this tape over and over again. If I was to move on from these patterns, I needed to create a new tape.

> Talking with him regarding breakup,
> I feel "hole" on top of my head
> downloading white electricity,
> lifting me upward in detachment—
> from him and circumstance.

I was learning detachment at the same time I was enmeshed. One night at a dance, I watched him "coming on" to another woman. I was crushed, my insecurity that of a teenager. Journeys with angels and spirit beings had not healed wounds of my psyche. I had to change by going deeper into unconscious patterns, beliefs, and behaviors. That change came through living life and learning from its ups and downs, bumps, and bruises.

> He pours it on
> feeding ego appetite.
> She catches the bait
> riding the wave
> and I crash on shore
> drowned in feelings of
> betrayal, abandonment, isolation.

I left him to return, and then left again. I attended counseling sessions, read self-help books, and tried to stay away, but I was not healthy enough to take this sensible step, nor had I learned to change myself instead of playing the blame game. He and I were codependent in dysfunction and addicted to hot honeymoon phases. It was a merry-go-round of breaking up to get back together—round and round—again and again. I was trapped in my own confusion. With the assistance of a counselor, I faced my issues and eventually discovered the appropriate mantra for well-being: "Get a life."

> Nonattachment to men
> I hold the cards,
> control my life,
> choosing to balance it
> with a variety of friends and activities.
> My world of choice expands.

One night after months of yet another separation, I invited him to my apartment. I had lost a few pounds, wore a slinky black dress, and felt quite frisky. We made crazy love. The next morning after he left, sparkling golden hues poured softly into the room and a distinct energetic presence took the shape of a Greek Goddess. She beamed waves of subtle yellows and reds, whispering, "Gabrielle." Why does an angelic Goddess appear after a wild night of lovemaking? Angels of Light must also be angels of Earth.

He and I had different interests. I wanted to camp in the wilderness rather than golf on manicured greens, eat in funky ethnic restaurants rather than fine dining, dance country rather than ballroom, and meditate at sacred sites rather than drive through towns like a tourist in Ireland, Mexico, and Hawaii. He thought it odd that I wanted to display a flag of the planet outside our home along the country club's golf course. He was a citizen of the USA; I was a global citizen. He was conservative; I was liberal. How do such opposites attract? The answer seems simple: to learn the lessons we came to learn, working out karma from previous lives. We eventually married and that cycle of yet another honeymoon lasted only a short time.

I wrote the following poem in April 1999 and left the relationship in November 2000.

> Spider web woven
> with sexual strands of magnetic potion.
> Spider beguiling wanting his prey, needing his feast.
> Ah! Here's a victim so pretty in pink.
> Eyes glazing, force oozing, he strikes.
> They seldom resist, captivated by seduction.
> For the moment it satisfies,
> for the moment it distracts,
> but it's never enough.

> He's on watch once again, obsessing.
> I grow weary of the repetitive scene
> observed from my place on the sticky web
> bouncing me this way and that.
> One day, I will escape this web
> and the poison we weave.
> One day, I will be free.

Our relationship was sexually charged. He was an excellent lover and knew how to please me through poetry reading, sweet pillow talk, laughter, and multiple orgasms. After lovemaking I often had out-of-body tantric experiences taking me to other realms. According to author Barbara Tedlock, PhD, in *The Woman in the Shaman's Body*, (Bantam Books/March/2005), "Sexually ecstatic states are celebrated literally as well as symbolically in tantric and Kundalini yoga, both of which evolved out of north Asian Shamanic practices."

Tantra, a Sanskrit word, comes from the root *tan,* meaning "to weave," and is the experience of weaving physical *and* spiritual substance within oneself and with a partner. This union is divine, giving sexuality expanded dimension.

Tantric visions with my husband often revealed Native Americans, who I sensed (the elusive faces never spoke) were connected to the spirit of the land we lived on, Pacific Cascadia, a bioregional term for the Pacific Northwest. Once I envisioned him wearing an Indian breastplate; another time I saw him as chief with full-feathered headdress. I told him my experiences as they unfolded and he listened openly. He gave himself the name "Two Cats" in honor of the visions and his two Siamese cats. We both sensed that we had been together in a past life.

Like a raging fire, my sexuality was at its peak, especially during ovulation. This powerful hormonal chemistry requires personal boundaries in order to keep it in check in an intelligent and sacred way.

Light of Fertility Moon

Monthly phase of ovulation turns me into a different woman. Like a werewolf under full moon, I become aggressive. My skin feels like iron pilings, drawn and raised by a magnet. I wear magnetic fur. Ovaries cramping, discharging, I am on the hunt. Sexual fantasies come alive as I wander land of erotica. Is this a nightmare that frightens? Is this a monster out of control?

No! I am Goddess! I wear golden robes of energetic Light. I embrace this Light of fertility and release it with passionate power. I release—earth quaking; I release—water flowing; I release—fire burning; I release—wind spiraling. Earth, water, fire, air, alive and moving through this body.

Magnetism is in my cells, a force of nature. I open to this natural force and let it move me through the terrain of my daily life. I welcome my wild nature and how it enlivens my world, as does moon in her magnetic full force. Knowing magnetic rhythms of earth body, I know wholeness in a holy place. Here is power. Here is grace.

Sexual energy with its red/orange vibrational color did not keep our relationship and marriage alive. We were missing yellow's personal empowerment, green's compassion, and blue's honest communication. We did not find the pot of gold at the end of the rainbow, and the fire burned out.

What lessons did I learn? I learned not to be codependent and a woman who loves too much. I learned healthy boundaries and not to give up personal identity and interests for a man.

> Relationship is like a pail of water.
> It works when there are no holes.

> Every part of this soil is sacred in the estimation of my people. Every hillside, every valley, every plain and grove, has been hallowed by some sad or happy event in days long vanished.
>
> —Chief Seattle, *This Sacred Soil*

Chapter 13

Serpent Sacred

Reviewing my writings I notice how "snake" or "serpent" has played a significant role in my mystical journey through dreams, visions, and my garden. I did not seek or choose these mystical beings, they chose me by showing up for me.

Sacred Soil

I value snake and serpent symbolically for their ancient role in Goddess religions and their close proximity to Mother Earth's rich brown soil—sacred soil that holds and feeds all life. Serpent is my totem and guide through dreamtime and shamanic time. Serpent is my friend in this linear time.

Serpent Dream

I am walking with a man who is taller than I am. We see a snake. It wants to get close to me and I freak out—a physical snake is different from a mystical one. It wraps around my neck and I consciously work to stay calm. I focus and attune to the snake. I feel its presence around my neck moving left to right, then hear it make a sharp sound at, and then in, my right ear. The man unwraps the snake from my neck very carefully because it's tangled in my hair. He lifts the snake high. I think he's going to throw it but he gently places it on the ground. The man then strokes my head and neck.

Serpent Journey

The 2007 planning council for the Faery and Human Relations Congress held intention to connect with nature spirits and devas at Skalitude Retreat Center in north-central Washington. As part of this visioning process and shamanic journey I experienced the following:

Serpentine line moves as one and then there are two. I ask, "Is serpent similar to faery?" Then wings appear and… dragon! I am on dragon's back, flying in a circle. Serpent and I come face-to-face; we look at each other and kiss.

Serpent and dragon lines are mysterious and difficult to grasp with left, linear brain. I sense their association with ley lines, energy grids, dowsing, constellation Draco, Kundalini, England, Grand Canyon, Costa Rica, underworld, feng shui, and Chinese medicine. These spiritual spaces and physical places are connected via lines that meander through humankind's ancient memory. Snake, serpent, and dragon are part of our lineage. Do we remember in fear or in reverence? Do we remember these missing parts of ourselves?

Serpent Sacred

One morning my "household" of emotional, mental, and physical bodies woke up to an etheric serpent slithering north and south, showing healthy and firm belly. We felt inclined to sensually slither and intertwine in response. We are cautious, however, in these mystical realms due to manipulative ways of an evil sorcerer (yes, in this realm.). We chose, instead, to watch and listen. Serpent then appeared with its head cut off and limp body hanging. We watched and listened some more. Serpent was now intact, alive, and seemed to be part of us—skin like. Later in a moment of stillness, serpent dream explained: Goddess head and body had been severed, separated. Another God/dess force moves, full bodied and whole in this world, announcing green fertility—a safe place for beings of all realms.

Serpent Brain

It is said that humans have a reptilian brain. Does this mean I once coiled on rock in heat of sun and slithered along the ground darting through crevices, decaying leaves and tall grasses? Does this mean I shed my skin and gripped my prey with powerful jaws? I like the thought of being that primal and close with Mother Earth.

Snake Friend

I saw a garter snake near my river today. The last snake I saw was in my house after I left a door open for several hours one summer evening. It must have preferred my home to the horse pasture. I like snakes. When I was young, I would often see them as I biked on country roads. I was happy when I could nudge them off the road for their safety.

Snake Medicine

Gardening is a great opportunity to encounter snakes. I once managed a community garden that was circular in design and overgrown with mustard, reed canary grass, and thistle. One spring as I was clearing a section for sowing of seed, I found a twenty-three-inch snakeskin, intact from head to tail. I was elated and grateful that I had said *no* to the men wanting to use machinery to plow the garden. This "gift" is on my altar with other medicine. Yes, medicine people have "power animals" in this realm and in the etheric realm who choose us to work with them for the larger good. We keep an eye open for these spirit allies and their gifts, never taking them for granted. Like snake, we steer by scent. Our value is of earth, our pheromone of wind and rain, our habitat under sun, moon, and stars

Snake as Goddess

It is said snake is symbolic of Goddess, the female creative power found in all of the oldest traditions and religions. That feminine force of nature—my nature and your nature. Let's revisit snake of old and erase the fear that surrounds this ancient and mystical being. Let's invite her into our dreams and visions. Let's listen to her stories and watch for her signs. She's been listening and watching us for a long, long time.

Snake Tribute

Years ago, I wrote a poem about a snake that I encountered one afternoon while playing golf.

> I see you, O' Snake,
> wiggly, squiggly on this fairway green.
> I used to see you often, as a child
> in pasture green dotted with ant hill
> on pavement hot bicycling by.
> Today we meet, two creatures in time
> startled and frozen eye to eye.
> You wrap around in serpentine design,
> heart shaped on carpet Earth,
> symbol of Goddess with so much to say.

We be light, we be life, we be fire! We sing electric flame, we rumble underground, we dance heaven! Come be we and be free!

—Kate Griffin, *A Madness of Angels*

Chapter 14

Ecstatic Dance ~ A Story

I met like-minded and like-hearted women at the annual Faery and Human Relations Congress and enjoyed blossoming friendships. One evening a few of us agreed to meet in Seattle to go dancing.

Bells. She must wear bells... on her right ankle. So she threads blue-green beads and silver bells attaching a silver clasp. "Was Tinker Bell behind this?" she wondered.

A large circle of people surrounds the dance floor. There is talk about sacred space and setting intention through dance. She is impatient with the words but accepts the process. Gradually a single chime stirs the crowd.

Free-form movement begins, quietly at first. "World-beat" music lifts the crowd into increasing complexity. Dancers attune to tempo, quickening their pace in flowing skirts, hip scarves, tribal fusion, and yoga pants, weaving a colorful parade. Belly-dance undulations honor the feminine; strong strides speak for the masculine.

Drums beat. Couples move skillfully and erotically, two becoming one ecstatic body, unlike anything she has seen on ballroom or country dance floors. Musical impulses spark her body into motion. She yields to her own trance of ecstasy that fuels her fire and feeds her joy.

In the midst of trance, she is grabbed by the shoulders. A Faery Congress sister makes contact, then a second! They had found each other in the crowd. The three dance joyfully holding hands, making their own merriment and fairy ring: one woman with a new boyfriend, the other planning a wedding, and she with happy bells tinkling.

A man in wild native dress with a lot of skin showing meanders through the crowd and stops near them. He gyrates with a partner, smiling at the fairy sisters with a twinkle of mischief in his eye. Then he steps toward her and holds out his hand. She reaches out and receives... a feather.

In the midst of ecstatic trance dance, she is touched by the feathery wild.

> The light shed by any good relationship illuminates all relationships.
>
> —Anne Morrow Lindbergh, *Gift from the Sea*

Chapter 15
Telepathic Relationships

Over the past fourteen-years I have experienced long-distance relationships, so distant that they were telepathic. These relationships fascinated me as much as they frustrated me.

One day, after months of visionary experiences, my thoughts about a certain man took a quantum leap, and in a split second, I saw him in his house—as if I were there! I was taken aback by this sudden teleportation into someone's personal space. "What door in my mind just opened?" I wondered. "What trick is my mind playing?" I pondered. Etheric encounters with angels, fairies, serpents, and dragons were mystical. I was comfortable with that. This earth plane human encounter was not the same. I felt vulnerable being in his house. Did he know I was there? Did anyone see me? I was in unknown territory. Did this remote viewing or second sight mean I was telepathic? The term wasn't important to me. I was *seeing*—a verb more experientially powerful than any noun to name it.

> *Telepathy is the energetic transfer of touch, ideas, thoughts, emotions, feelings and sound. A telepathic connection is the energy bond that connects two or more minds into the same energetic wave length to utilize telepathy.*

> *We broadcast emotions, moods, thoughts, attitudes, fragments of our personality unknowingly every day. Everything that emits energy also absorbs energy. Meaning, that with practice we can learn to read and speak to one another without ever moving our mouths!*
> —www.outofbodyecstasy.com/telepathic-sex/

A couple of years later, I experienced my body as a radar screen, picking up energetic signals from a particular man whose vibrations "pinged" my energy field, or aura, at my lowest chakras with red/orange sexuality. This man projected these "vibes" toward me all times of day and night but would not speak with me publicly or privately. Though these hot and cold messages were confusing, I thought, as most women do, that sexual attraction was associated with love. As a result, I engaged in my first sexually charged telepathic relationship. No one knew; it was a secret. It was also infuriating until I let go of the old brainwashing pattern of being drawn by red/orange sexual energy and moved on.

Personal relationships with men have been stepping-stones for me, one leading to the next, each one offering new lessons and awareness. The next man I was attracted to emitted animal magnetism. His vibrational frequency came in at my crown chakra as subtle waves, washing over me sensually, with a sweet integrating force that aroused my lower chakras. This new quality of contact took me deeper into tantra, with Kundalini fire resounding through my core, enlivening my whole chakra system. This was a whole body-mind-spirit experience that took telepathic sex to a new level. Instead of only red/orange cylinders firing, this relationship ignited my whole circuitry!

Telepathic sex occurs when one person reaches out to another energetically, mind to mind. Intention paves the way. My body informs me when someone is thinking of me, reaching out to me, intentionally. My body receives the transmission of sexual energy at my first and second chakra; loving energy at my green heart chakra; and spiritual energy at my crown chakra. This communication is experienced "out of body" through the energy body, or aura, as the five physical senses (sight, sound, taste, touch, and smell) become passive. A more subtle sense comes into play as two people tune in and listen as one—giving and receiving cues through long distance communication.

As two people reach out emotionally and mentally, their projected energy meets in the middle to create a third "holographic" field suspended in space. Here sexual passion rises and falls as waves of subtle electric currents run through one's body. For me telepathic sex was "tantra sacred" as Kundalini's fiery current whiplashed upward through my spine with such force that my head was thrown backward—the ultimate dragon surrender. This extraordinary, extrasensory fire-dragon bliss came alive in 2005.

> Fire dragon lives at the core—
> my core, your core, Earth's core.
> Fire dragon breathes from the core—
> my core, your core, Earth's core.
> Fire dragon speaks through skin—
> my skin, your skin, Earth's skin.
> An electromagnetic force,
> fire dragon lives E/S/W/N,
> me to you, you to me, people to Earth.
> Fire dragon radiates love
> to earth, through Earth, on Earth.
> Goddess smiles.

This relationship was similar to the previous telepathic relationship. Both men communicated telepathically without verbal communication or physical touch. Imagine fiery passion playing out in telepathic realms, yet in this physical realm the partner is not available. Imagine relating intimately in the dark, in secret, and not expressing thoughts or feelings in the light of day. Where were the other elements of water, air, and earth? This way of relating worked for the men (who had other partners), it did not work for me. Weaving throughout this relationship something new emerged—my Sacred Masculine—protecting my Sacred Feminine, informing me it was time to set logical boundaries. This inner support assisted me in letting go and moving on, once again.

Why was I attracted to men who were not available in a grounded and healthy way? Enter childhood with a father and mother who did not talk about feelings. Enter lack of emotional connection and, thus, lack of emotional intelligence. What was my lesson? Was it to learn unconditional love? Was it to radiate love without concern for results, my ongoing mantra? Those are great spiritual concepts but it wasn't what my heart, mind, and body wanted. Feedback is critical for a relationship to thrive, and feedback includes the physical realm. When my inner masculine logic and feminine feeling aligned in intelligence, I was able to move out of the pattern of engaging in telepathic relationships.

Yet there is more to this story. There is always larger context and meaning in which our dramas play out here on earth. The larger story: these telepathic relationships were lessons in transcending physical relationships. The men provided points of external focus as my feminine and masculine evolved internally. Telepathic relationship is similar to having a distant planet or star in one's orbital field and relating, orb to orb, through inner senses. The men represented positive sun and I represented negative, receptive earth. The absorption and emission of electromagnetic currents generated a force field (something I could press into and relate to) bringing many spiritual insights, and providing substance for me to spin and evolve cycle after cycle.

Winter Solstice

Sun lover,
your touch is thin.
I beseech your return

> closer, closer to me.
> Fire my core.
> Encircle my body.
> Warm my atmosphere.
> Arouse my soil,
> Penetrate my roots.
> In winter's darkest hour,
> Light of love returns.

How prevalent is telepathic relationship and telepathic sex? How many people are relating mind-to-mind, heart-to-heart and spirit-to-spirit without physical touch? I invite you to tell me your story of this relationship phenomenon so together we can bring this experience out of the dark and into light of greater consciousness.

I also wish to alert women who are doing inner spiritual work that there are men who prey on women telepathically. These men may look like inspirational and spiritual leaders, medicine men, and shamans, but underneath their titles and roles, they are stuck in the lowest chakras. If you let these men into your energetic space, some might take advantage and assault you psychically. This manipulative and controlling behavior is not from a vibrational green chakra heart. Some of these men might be sociopaths or sex addicts who feed off women. So be aware! If you are looking for that absent father or have low self-esteem, you might be inclined to fall for them. To evolve beyond limiting childhood issues and low-chakra behavior patterns, don't go there. These predators could also be unbalanced emotionally and stalk and harass you—for years—while no one believes you when you tell the story. Let this be a warning from one who knows. This is the shadow side of telepathic experience. I am told there are women who also walk this path in telepathic and shamanic realms. I, however, have met only men who do this.

The good news is that I evolved! My inner female is now relating to my inner male, two opposites engaged in healthy communion (soul-to-soul) and communication (heart-to-mind). This intelligence assists in setting healthy boundaries.

Love I Am

*Sun substance pours freely
into fields of relationships.
Some respond with color displays,
some remain barren,
with no capacity to bloom and grow.
Fields matter not; sun matters.*

Throughout my life, I related to men as potential lovers. In early 2014, I became interested in relating to men as friends, building relationship based on spiritual intimacy that included spending time together and sharing honest thoughts and feelings. My inner female and male were now experiencing friendship. Could my outer world reflect the same? One man I spent time with told me that men cannot only be friends—that he needed to have sex with a woman to really know her. This did not resonate with me at all! I discovered that some men weren't interested in friendship, and I felt repelled rather than attracted. Other men wanted a lot of my time and their energy felt needy. The mantra, "Get a life," from my previous codependent relationship was in play. Now living a full and active life, I no longer needed a man to make me happy and whole.

I wanted to build friendship through spiritual intimacy first; men wanted to have sex before friendship. In looking at this discrepancy of wants I realized that I had evolved! I now wanted men to relate to my Light body first and my physical body second. This insight informed me that S/He Dragon *was* my Light Body! This breakthrough in consciousness was like the sun peeking through dark clouds. I now knew myself better!

> Cease trying to work everything out in your mind.
> It will get you nowhere. Live by intuition and
> inspiration and let your whole life be revelation.
>
> —*Eileen Caddy*

Chapter 16
River of Life ~ A Teaching

In the Cascade wilderness of Washington State I stood beside a wild river. In the middle of its swift currents a large snag held a collection of logs, branches and long grasses. This log jam changed the river's story and conveyed a simple teaching.

There are snags in the river of life obstructing its flow. There are a number of choices in response.

— Ignore the snag.
— Deny that the snag exists.
— Analyze and intellectualize the snag from all angles.
— Tell stories about the snag (front page "news").
— Blame someone for the snag.
— Support the snag, keeping it alive.

These responses sustain the snag, carrying it forward in the river of life as a navigational burden. The burden will, sooner or later, dam up the entire river. A snag can be negative attitudes, addictions, codependent relationships, cancer in the body, polluted rivers, or vanishing bees. Snags stop the natural flow.

There are a number of solutions in response.

- Look and see the snag.
- Acknowledge that the snag exists.
- Get to the root of the snag.
- Take the drama out of the snag.
- Take personal responsibility for the snag.
- Let go of the snag, take new action, and heal.

Am I willing to choose—and be—the solution? Are we, as citizens of community, country, and planet willing?

What we are doing to the forests of the world is but a mirror reflection of what we are doing to ourselves and to one another.

—Mahatma Gandhi

Chapter 17

Wilderness Awareness

After my second divorce, in November 2000, I moved north to spend more time in nature. For years, I had let go of personal interests and activities for "my man." Golfing, ballroom dancing, fine dining, and country club conversations did not feed my pagan soul. Now I wanted to ground in earth under sky and stars. Here are "nature clips" from those moments in time when I immersed in nature. Each bird, animal and plant I saw, every sound and movement I heard, the contours of land I felt under my feet, the earthy scents and tastes of nature made impressions on my brain-body. As nature sang her song of being, I followed along, letting her ground me. The missing brain-body parts I had lost years earlier with Kundalini's snap, were returning.

Pipe Smoke

I wander eastward uphill along the Tolt Trail as setting sun behind me kisses earth good-night. A towhee with black hood, reddish brown flanks, and tail feathers streaked white perches nearby. One sings to another, companion calling from Cedar's lacy greenery. Textures of the moment impress my senses as I am lifted by a mist of Native American pipe smoke—a gift from another realm or from this land that I am rooted in?

Tracking Club

Tracking Club drives to the sand bar to "track the landscape." Yellow wildflowers call and deer tracks beckon. Looking downward, locating, and analyzing animal tracks with scientific precision does not appeal to my right-brain orientation that sees the whole rather than detailed parts. I scout for trails and cozy, dry spots canopied with green. Earthy scents fill my nostrils and pores, enlivening.

Secret Spot

I walk to my secret spot along the River Sammamish, nibbling on tender young dandelion leaves for my daily dose of nutrients. Barn swallow nests, sculpted with mud and straw, are plastered under the eaves of a shop next to the horse pasture. Song sparrow sings with a sharp, clear shrill. Approaching the river, a great blue heron lifts on large wings, flying south. Is that an American goldfinch or a yellow warbler? It has black on its head. I identify it later thanks to *Peterson's Field Guide*.

Geese Parade

Geese fly in V formation, creating a sky parade with adults in front, alongside, and in the rear, guarding their yellowed young. This tight family, wearing what looks like long black stockings on their necks, wings their way through space. Adults gesture with linguistic purpose, teaching lines of community to their young. Landing downriver, they ease their ranks, tugging at tall grasses along the banks and dipping their beaks into slow-moving water. I watch and take it all in through a deep inhale of breath. "Ah." Absorbing—capturing and transforming energy—I am one. Am I absorbed through geese, are geese absorbed through me, or do we absorb each other in oneness that simply is this web of life?

Camp Don Bosco

At Camp Don Bosco, I crawl along the forest floor in a game of capture the flag, feeling a new bond with earth. I have permission to be a child again, getting dirt on my clothing and under painted fingernails. I have my "medicine" with me—sage, lavender, and cornmeal—to make offerings as I am called. My head feels light; my body feels sensual, erotic. I hear bird alarms in a line behind me… Hawk flies out on my right. There… a bird nest low to the ground—in a fern! Sweet! A mud fight ends our day of childlike innocence.

Voices of Spring

Morning bike ride, in tune with spring. What is that? A movement! A tiny beak, then another! Barn swallow nests are full of activity as the parents dance their forked tail signature of sweeping joy across the sky. I walk to the weeping willows near Grandmother Black Cottonwood, and then stop to sit in silence. A male common yellowthroat appears with black mask. This four-inch being sings, "Witchery, witchery, witchery." Walking home, I see a large flock of blackbirds pecking for food in the field. The birds in back leapfrog to the front, creating a rhythmic circulating motion as everyone is fed. I feel attuned, on wings of peaceful synchronicity.

First Steps

Little hands wrap around my fingers as we take her first stair steps. Up, down, up, down, giggling all the way. Such is Granddaughter Sierra's joy in self-discovery.

Forest Life

Orange-mouthed salmonberry flowers vocalize their song. Walking the forest absorbing scents, I look down and see a three-by-three-inch track in mud. I sketch the impressions of the front and hind feet in my journal to identify them later. A black mouse-like critter scurries out from the leaf litter, led by its fleshy nose. An American shrew mole (*Neurotrichus gibbsi*)? Inner ears hear trees say, "Don't dissect me in pieces with logical mind. Leave me whole, and hear my song." Under canopy of fir, maple, and cedar, the landscape dips into a creek with a hidden hollow and den. I catch the scent of fairy!

Dawn Chorus

At the river, 5:30 a.m. I am mesmerized by the birds' melodious dawn chorus, offering thanksgiving for a new day. A bullfrog roars loudly; another responds farther out. A field of yellow tall buttercup and dandelion awakens to the flight of a yellow warbler and a common yellowthroat. Summer wears her glory gown.

Tracking the Landscape

Two fallen trees bear the markings of beaver's chew; flicker is on my right; robin walks with me down the path then takes a buoyant hop toward me (reminding me of Emily Dickinson's poem "A Bird Came down the Walk"); wild trillium is in white bloom; maple tree has a mouse house!

Nettle Field

Stinging nettle field emits pungent earthy fragrance. I "swim" through it, parting the five-foot native plants with breaststroke motions. Long jeans, boots, and sleeves pulled over hands protect me from the infamous stinging hairs on leaves and stems. My destination is the blackberry thicket where I clear a tunnel to make myself invisible to this world. Is this tunnel a birth canal? What am I birthing? What is birthing me?

Zen Lesson

Yesterday I effortlessly climbed a fir tree. Today mind interferes with fear and doubt, but I climbed that tree anyway. Zen lesson: Still mind clears the way for action. Fearful mind holds one back. Red clover calls. I ask permission and gather their flowers to dry for tea, leaving more than I pick. I extend gratitude.

Poplar Dance

It is 4:30 a.m. Poplar trees dance with wind, interacting sensually, like lovers. I watch from my personal plot of earth, conscious of my presence in this larger whole. It is a privilege to watch the elements of water, air, earth and fire interact in their emotional love affair. I have nowhere to go, nothing to achieve. Last quarter moon peeks through cloudy sky.

Morning Glory

It is 8:00 a.m. Sun rays warm my spine and neck as I walk to the river. A dove roosts under the bridge. At my feet a stellar jay feather says "hello," and a sparrow sings, tilting its head back as if gargling rich, round notes. Ducks swim happily, followed by yellow goslings. A wren plucks cattail fluff, singing in flight as she builds her nest, camouflaged in tall grass. Nature, full of animation, makes me feel connected and alive.

Elfin Nation

I stop pedaling and set my bike down. Dandelions catch my attention and I eat their tender leaves. Tiny orbed mushrooms, gray and brown, greet me with elfin images of another dimension: Pointy feet, ears, and hat "download" a message to me: "We, Elfin Nation, create a network underfoot, and we ground electricity."

Underground

Cedar tree calls. I wander past bird's nest, rabbit scat, and an underground burrow system. I too want to travel underground as grief rises up at my human limitation. Great blue heron's voice is raucous, his antics graceful, on the water's edge. Another heron poised on one long leg hunts for food under the bridge. Red-tail hawk keeps me company. I enter an altered state—my personal burrowing route underground.

Summer Winds Down

Beehive activity of summer winds down. My pace relaxes with the cooling of night air. This turning of season is cozy and reassuring in its consistent cycle of change.

Moon Lodge

Eight females gather to celebrate Grandmother Moon in her fullness. I feel warm this crisp, clear night at Mosswood Hollow. Chili relleno casserole, cinnamon bread, and salad nurture stomachs and hearts inside the cozy, warm yurt embraced by maple, cedar, and fir trees. Candles encircle us, flickering; more candles to be taken home. I choose a purple one that signifies, "Transition, spiritual awakening, and dream state." Moonlit ferns shimmer and share sisterhood. Rattles and drums reverberate; earth chants rise as we dance around apple tree, paying tribute to Grandmother Moon, Goddess, and the Ancestors.

Misfit

I hear *crunch, crunch* of leaf litter and grass under foot at 6:00 a.m. Smoke rises from the local brewery in winter's cold and the pungent scent of hops is unmistakable. Hawk screeches... once. Stars are bright, their names unknown. Does it matter? Intuitive knowing cannot stand alone; detailed logic alone cannot stand. One needs the other for intelligence—a balanced, two-way path.

How does my right-brain fit into this left-brain world? I'm told I can learn to remember facts and information if I want, if I try. Does that say something is wrong with me? I feel grief. Am I a misfit because it's easier for me to have visions than to remember details?

Laughter

Laughing boulder, tickled by waters. Laughing fern, tickled by fairy wings. Laughing pine, tickled by wind. Laughing mountain, tickled by moonbeams. Laughing me, tickled by it all.

White Dragon

New relationship: White dragon appears with huge wings providing safety and protection when I journey in dreamtime and linear time.

Birthing My Drum

I birth my drum in Seattle's Women of Wisdom workshop with Starfeather. This creative process holds tranquility even when the rawhide cord breaks—three times! While tying the first knot, the image of a Celtic knot appears. Perhaps rawhide was telling its own story. I don't judge the breakage as negative (as some had suggested), but see it as part of the process.

Drum Journey

I drum and feel a brainwave shift in my head. Spirit animals gather around, along the edge, responding to drum call. Brook Medicine Eagle's *Gathering: The Sacred Breath* chants bring them through one at a time, species by species.

Welcome

My second grandchild, Parker, is born. Welcome little one.

> Some people awaken spiritually without ever coming into contact with any meditation technique or any spiritual teaching. They may awaken simply because they can't stand the suffering any more.
>
> —Eckhart Tolle

CHAPTER 18
MEDITATION SHORES

Meditation changed my life. It opened a window for my encounter with Archangel Michael and Light, and it revealed that slowing down, turning within, and being fully present in the moment allows me to access deep states of relaxation and consciousness. This source of inner peace stayed with me as I traveled through life's bumpy and smooth terrain.

One New Year's Eve, I went to a party with a friend. People were talking about their relationship issues. One woman said there were layers and layers of issues. I responded by saying this provided an opportunity to go to one's core. She looked at me, skeptical. In my healing journey I had created a meditative path to an inner sanctum of stillness. This core experience had, again and again, released stress from my daily life, helped me transcend drama, and wrapped me in a blanket of serenity.

One of my earliest meditations took place on a lakeshore in northern California. Letting go of my logical mind, with its chatter about past, present and future activity, I focused within, opening up to something larger than myself. Thoughts came and went, I let them pass without judgment. On the lake's surface spiraling ripples beckoned me into their mesmerizing patterns. In a deep meditative state I became one with water, lake, landscape, planet and cosmos.

Years later, in Ireland, another body of water mesmerized me.

Lake Killarney

> Waves crawl to the shore,
> I catch a wave to meditate upon.
> It ripples and spirals,
> through lifetimes of learning
> and learnings of a lifetime.
> Who is the teacher? Who is the student?
> We take turns, dancing.

Meditation is an opportunity to be receptive (feminine) instead of active (masculine). Receptive to what? In my experience, it is receptivity to Light, spiritual energy, allowing it to activate my field of energy and enter my house of physical matter. Becoming receptive and still can be a challenge for those of us who have a list of to-dos that can't wait until tomorrow or next week, those of us always "on the run." The rewards, however, are well worth it. Herbert Benson, MD, founder of the Mind/Body Institute at Harvard Medical School's Beth Israel Deaconess Medical Center states, "The relaxation response from meditation helps decrease metabolism, lowers blood pressure, and improves heart rate, breathing and brain waves." (www.webmd.com/balance/feautres/transcendental-meditation)

> Meditation as medication,
> open the mind and swallow.

The brain is made up of billions of cells called neurons, which use electricity to communicate with each other. This electrical activity is called a brainwave pattern, because of its cyclical, wave-like nature. "It

is well known that the brain is an electrochemical organ; researchers have speculated that a fully functioning brain can generate as much as 10 watts of electrical power. Electrical activity emanating from the brain is displayed in the form of brainwaves."
(www.web-us.com/brainwaves function.htm)

Four brainwaves, known as beta, alpha, theta, and delta, are measured through amplitude (how high and how low the waves travel compared to a straight line) and frequency (how many times per second the wave peaks).

Meditation takes me out of ordinary *beta brainwave* frequency (low amplitude/energy and fast in frequency) with its everyday logic and critical reasoning and into the relaxation, imagination, and visualization of *alpha brainwave* frequency (higher in amplitude and slower in frequency).

Drumming or rattling takes me deeper into inspiration, creativity, and insight with *theta brainwave* frequency (greater amplitude and even slower frequency).

Delta brainwaves are the slowest frequency. Active while I dream, they connect me with deeper parts of my unconscious mind.

When my brain shifts into a meditative, alpha state of consciousness I feel a passing pressure at the top of my head, and hear a subtle "click." Once, while watching a TV show about brain function, I heard the sound of this click. The scientists on the show described the sound as "neurons firing." Does "firing" include brainwave activity engaging chakras that, in turn, engage endocrine glands to release hormonal chemicals into my bloodstream, informing my nervous system? It does feel this way as sweet substance pours through the top of my head, downloading through my torso. I have come to know this substance that moves through my crown chakra as Light. This radiant force moving through my physiology is the union of Light energy and Dark matter. The sensation is lifting, the experience holy.

> Do you feel it?
> In your cells, blood, and bones?
> Do you feel it?
> Sweet influences
> seeping through pores?
> Light transforming
> matter.

I have often asked myself the question: "Is solar light, received through my physical eyes, the same as spiritual Light, received through my crown chakra when I close my eyes?" Are there two different types of Light or is sunlight captured and stored in different parts of our body to be utilized when needed?

> *Mystical and spiritual traditions from nearly every culture have linked the Sun to [hu]man's higher evolution. Cultures as diverse as the Essenes, The Mayan, Aztecs, Buddhists, Hindus, Oceanic Tribes, and Native Americans all link the power of the Sun to man's higher nature.*
> *The human eye is actually a miniature sun and like the sun of our solar system, it has the ability to absorb and radiate light. It absorbs energy through the retina from where it is redistributed to the brain and nervous system. We know that these energy particles are the carriers of various Universal Factors of Energy.*
> —www.spiritualharmonics.blogspot.com/2008/06/hidden-reality-of-solar-light.html

Posture and breathing is important while meditating, assisting the mind and body with relaxation, alertness, and presence. Sit still and up straight with your face, neck, back and shoulders relaxed, hands resting on the knees or in the lap. Good posture and deep breathing allows the chakras to receive brainwave electricity and pass this energy on to the body's life support systems: endocrine, nervous, circulatory, immune, lymphatic, digestive, muscular, reproductive, respiratory, skeletal and urinary. This system is Light's way of moving energy through the whole body engendering physical vitality.

I gravitate to cedar trees. Their upright trunk, scaly bark and lacy greenery call to me. I sit under their branching arms and meditate.

Dawn Meditation

> Grandmother cedar embraces me,
> walking away, I observe:
> core centered, eyes clear,
> legs strong, feet grounded,
> hands quiet, face beaming,
> lean and light.

> A gyroscope will always return to equilibrium however far it is pushed one way or the other.
>
> —George Orwell

Chapter 19
Gyroscope ~ Blog 2006

I created a blog years ago to record what was transpiring on my spiritual journey. Having that record allows me to look back and see how my life evolved as a moment-to-moment and day-to-day process, helps me remember details of that process, and tells my story through time. These blog entries capture inner reflections, "real time" encounters, and mystical journeys into multidimensions.

Tidal Shift

It's not enough to attend church and pray. It's not enough to meditate and do yoga. It's not enough to know the science of quantum physics. It's not enough to astral travel and meet spirit guides. It's not enough to find bliss in nature. It's not enough.

Enough begins when I excavate deep layers of my psyche. Enough is when I face my ghosts and demons, loosening and freeing them from their haunts. Enough is when I feel the deep wounds of emotional pain and grieve cycle by cycle.

Dark and Light go hand in hand. Spirit is just another word and spirituality is just another mental concept until I get dirty in the mud of my unconscious. Here my psyche is aerated and purged.

Turning away from darkness is not enough. Now is the time. This is the place. I am enough to face the Dark.

Global Brain

In *The Global Brain*, author Peter Russell shows that humanity has reached a crossroads in its evolutionary path. He asserts that the Internet is linking humanity into one worldwide community—a "global brain." This, combined with a rapidly growing spiritual awakening, is creating a collective consciousness that is humanity's only hope of saving itself from itself.

Gyroscope

There are times I feel that I am coming apart at the seams as my North/South axis tilts to an extreme degree. This outward spin takes me off balance, and, when I notice, consciously comes back in like an intense fiery current. Is this gyroscopic dance natural? Will it ever balance and stay in harmony? Or is chaos part of a harmonics spectrum that offers information?

Negative Backlash

Once I lived with a male partner and occasionally had negative feelings toward him. As a result, I created a neck injury. Thinking he was a "pain in the neck" manifested that very same pattern in my body. It was easier to blame him without looking within myself to see what was blocking my own positive life force from flowing. A counselor and self-help books assisted me in this process of taking personal responsibility and changing my negative thought pattern. Thoughts are powerful and create one's reality.

Love Account

At the local chapter of Institute of Noetic Sciences (IONS) we watched a video about the "science and practice of love" with Jeff Levin, PhD, and Frances Vaughn, PhD. I learned that Sanskrit has ninety-six words for *love*. Our Western language has very few words for love. Does this limit our experience of love?

A coworker inspires people to invest in positive words and actions by putting a penny in a jar for every positive expression and withdrawing a penny for every negative expression. This "love account" reveals a lot about one's personal investment of energy.

Loving energy acts like a laser beam cutting through darkness. Negative darkness wants to dance with positive light—in harmonious balance. Today is Valentine's Day! Let's embrace Dark and Light forces within and in the world around us. Let's allow the magic of love, all ninety-six types, to show us the way.

Charge / Discharge

I awake recharged, rising from the deep sleep of delta brainwave frequency, crossing theta and alpha brainwave, and grounding in daily consciousness of beta. Awakening often brings forward images, symbols or words giving me a clue as to what is unfolding in my consciousness and daily life. Today I sense energy moving as "charge and discharge." Charge is a filling up and from this fullness is discharge. The following stories reveal how this process showed up in my daily life.

My grandson, who is nearly two years old, was in the midst of a large group with an apprehensive look on his face. His eyes caught mine and he lit up! This discharge from him gave me a charge moving me to action: giving him a hug.

Moon Lodge Circle women discussed publishing an e-newsletter and I spontaneously announced that I wanted to write about fairies. Immediately, I sensed the presence of a large tree. Was the tree discharging energy in my field of awareness? This tree, seen through mind's eye, had roughly textured bark, and "hummed" in response. Tree liked my thought! At the end of the evening, we walked outside, and there, in front of me, stood a large western red cedar tree with that same rough bark. I "got" it! This was that tree! I walked up, put my back against it, engaged my whole being, and squealed to the other women, "This is that tree!" Energetic discharge and charge create relationship flow that has no boundaries and the emotional connection is outright *joy!* Our responsibility as conscious human beings is to keep energy flowing in a healthy balance of charge and discharge—and to recharge nightly with a deep dose of brainwaves.

Intimacy

Intimacy. What is it? What does it sound like, look like, feel like, taste like? I think intimacy sounds like a still alpine lake as well as a rushing rainforest waterfall; looks like multicolored hues dancing in space like the aurora borealis; feels like a warm bubble bath; tastes sweet like German chocolate cake, and smells like May lilac trees.

I, like most humans on this planet, was conditioned to think of intimacy as sexual in nature, involving the physical body. I have tried to find intimacy that way, but it has not manifested at a deep and meaningful level. For me, at this time in my life, spiritual intimacy takes priority. This includes the exchange of thoughts and feelings through a depth of honesty within myself. I consciously check my feelings to see if they are balanced with my logic. And I consciously check my thoughts to see if they are in synch with my feelings. This inner love affair keeps me "on my toes" through the honesty of intimacy.

Teeter-Totter

The sun streams morning rays, warming my living room. In golden stillness, I receive intuitive information and am inspired to discharge through communication. This blog relationship is a way for me to channel/release charged energy.

The question came in: "At what point?"

At what point does pleasant turn unpleasant, sweetness turn sour, kindness turn hurtful, fresh turn stagnant, and pretty turn ugly? The answer came through as a horizontal "8," a teeter-totter, with threads going through the center or "eye of needle." There was movement back and forth in a seesaw motion, indicating a range of energy, positive and negative. This equilibrium tells me to eat more rainbow chard and other living foods, to let go of drama, to do nothing, and to be still. "Be still and know that I am God/dess!" I notice new vibration in this still space. It is dynamic stillness—full and alive. That word *dominion* comes in again, a sign of hope as I enjoy the last of the chocolate and think about ice cream. Such a comical creature, this human that is finding her balance as a spiritual being. Wanna teeter-totter? My dad built a large teeter-totter when I was a child. It had two long boards joined and secured at the center. Four of us could sit, find balance, and go up high, down low, and around. Teeter-totters are fun!

Circuitry

The image "8" is pressing in on me, through mind's eye of intuition, telling me of its flowing circuitry, holding positive and negative charge. These two forces relate, giving and receiving energy, to keep a vital charge, circuit, and system alive. Is "8" the way currents move through my brain, chakras and body? Is "8" an echo chamber resounding as feedback loops, extending my energy into the world and bringing back to me an echoing pattern? The answers are fluid as the flow of "8" and cannot be processed by beta brainwave.

Love and Evol

Speaking truth within oneself and with others makes waves—waves of change. This warrior's journey can leave one in darkness with grief and loss. Light transmutes darkness. It takes time. Some say lifetimes. So why judge oneself or others? We are all traveling the same evolutionary path. Let's continue to evolve by asking ourselves new questions and expanding our capacity for new answers. We do this dynamic work together as one people and one planet—through the natural law of love/evol. Let's turn up the love!

Written in the hope that a time will come for all people that whenever they see a body they will also see a sacred soul.

—Charlotte S. Kasl, *Women, Sex, and Addiction*

Chapter 20

Body and Soul

My grandmother and mother were very overweight. I watched Mom attempt one diet after another, and purchase machinery that (while lying on it) moved the body, supposedly trimming body fat. Mom was too busy taking care of six children to go for walks or exercise. My older sister was self-conscious about her weight and never content with her appearance. These childhood role-models contributed to an early negative self-image about my body.

Weighing 104 pounds in third grade (the average weight was fifty to sixty pounds), I stood out as "Fatty Patty." When my dad and siblings went hiking in the mountains, I dreaded the steep climbs and being the one who lagged behind. I shunned volleyball and baseball at school, keeping a safe distance so I wouldn't feel embarrassed. Shopping for school clothes, an activity most young girls find delightful, mortified me as I walked to the back of department stores looking for size XX. At this young age, I was painted with a brush of insecurity and self-consciousness. Shame was the primer under it all.

Sucking my thumb soothed me as a child, and I suspect this habit began in the womb. In addition, I rubbed a piece of purple silk material on my nose—until fourth grade! I was very attached to this sensual stimulus and resisted the pressure from my parents to let go of this habit. When I succumbed to "growing up" and letting go of thumb sucking and my "silky," I found the perfect substitute: food!

I loved food then, and I love food now. Mom was a good cook, and I especially enjoyed her comforting casseroles, homemade rolls, and desserts that included flakey, buttery piecrusts hugging apples, blackberries, and rhubarb cream. The candy store at the corner was a regular stop with choices of Hostess Twinkies, candy bars, and ice cream. We ate three meals a day, including all the food groups, but I felt undernourished. I craved "Davy Crockett" bread, new in the stores, with hints of grains and "brown stuff" unlike the white Wonder Bread that was the staple at the time. And I craved parsley. At the Poodle Dog restaurant in Fife, enjoying fish and chips, I asked my siblings for the green garnish peeking out from the side of their plates. My body sent its own messages for nutrition.

Through my first marriage and raising a family, I continued to cook the all-American diet of meat, potatoes, cooked vegetables, and dessert. Then my body revolted. Though I was working out at a gym, I felt sluggish and stagnant at my solar plexus. I consulted a naturopath who suggested that the food I ate wasn't digesting properly. He introduced me to yogurt, tofu, hummus, and rice cakes and was adamant about fresh fruit and vegetables. He determined that my cravings of flour and sugar were the exact foods causing allergic reaction. My children were not thrilled with my new way of eating, commenting to this day about alfalfa sprouts growing in a jar on the windowsill and added to peanut butter sandwiches.

Gradually, my diet and cooking was inspired by Adelle Davis's *Let's Cook It Right,* Frances Moore Lappe's *Diet for a Small Planet,* Mollie Katzen's infamous *Moosewood Cookbook,* and Vicki Rae Chelf's *Cooking with the Right Side of the Brain.* These cookbooks provide a variety of delicious recipes supporting nutritional health for humans and ecological balance for the planet. Mom's cookbook, written for the ladies auxiliary of our local fire district #9, holds a special place next to these favorites on the kitchen shelf, ready to dish out recipes for comfort food.

My cookbook shelf continues to expand reflecting my changing awareness, emotional resilience (dessert recipes are diminishing), and nutritional needs. That expansion includes Ayurvedic, anti-inflammation, and raw foods. For years I stated that I preferred to eat my fruits and vegetables. Now, I juice in the morning and enjoy hearing my body say "thank you" for the vitality of organic lemon, beet, chard, cucumber, carrot, and ginger. There are so many delicious and nutritious combinations to feed to the juicer and oneself.

Food is a primary relationship in my life. It is a teacher and I continue to learn from its web of cellular memory wrapped in senses, emotions, nerves, muscles, and taste buds. Food gives me comfort and pleasure; I know how to relate to it compulsively. What does that look like? For me it's not sitting down and eating a package of cookies at one time or eating cake and doughnuts day after day. For me it's cyclical. I enjoy nutritious foods and then I dive into craving this empty food and that. I think of it as a chemical pattern that keeps my brain-body wobbling in pH imbalance. Did Mom's depression and emotional eating influence my erratic relationship with food early in the womb? Did Dad's disassociation with feelings create my never-ending hunger for sweets? Was food a substitute for nourishing personal connection?

I also remember being in my bedroom as a teenager and someone walking outside past the window making a cat call whistle. At the time I wondered if it was Dad. I still wonder. Being treated like an object left holes in the soil of my psyche and the soul of my spirit. It left me empty, hungry. As I learn to eat food that is alive and healing I also learn to heal missing parts of myself.

When I reflect back on feelings about my body I remember saying to dad: "Stop talking to me that way. I am your daughter!" I had been preparing for this moment in my mind and it arrived—at age forty! Years of buried hurt rose up and released from my deep subconscious as a grounding electrical charge surged through my body. I felt empowered! This warrior woman had found her voice adding to a collective voice of empowered women who stand up and speak their truth!

When I eat processed, lifeless foods, I become acidic and tilted, off balance. The gyroscopic sensation carries waves of heat throughout my body—inflammation. According to www.AcidAlkalineDiet.com: "On a whole, the average western diet is acid-producing. And when acidic wastes accumulate, they can cause organs to malfunction and break down."

I am responsible for making nutritional adjustments and pulling myself back into alignment. I learn what foods to eat, when to eat, how much to eat, and why a calm, peaceful atmosphere assists the process of healthy assimilation. That means no nibbling standing at the kitchen counter, and no mindless eating on the run! As my relationship path with food gets increasingly clear I cannot get away with old habits that create imbalance. I continue to listen to my body's intelligence as I work to stay in a pH zone of healthy equilibrium.

Personal feelings, thoughts, and actions are nutrients, providing nourishment essential for growth and the support of life. They, too, are acidic and alkaline, creating disease or health.

> Out of balance,
> eating though not hungry
> and critical self-talk.
> I take the reigns
> giving negative forces
> perspective and distance.
> The old is dying;
> something new is being born.

Understanding my relationship with food is a journey into dark unconscious territory. I need tools and skills to confront toxic demons that want control. I'm not battling the demons, however. I'm dancing with them as they alert me with inflammation and give me the opportunity to learn healthy boundaries. Sometimes, in frustration, I think I'd like to kill those demons, but that is not my nature. Toxins have had a stronghold and love their territory. This mirrors the larger body of humankind with demons holding toxic territory through violence and war. We learn to tame the toxic beasts through negotiation and dialogue, not war. And we learn from multidimensional spirit guides.

> In that magical hour between dark and dawn,
> a face appears with round ball of a nose.
> "Balboa" urges me to drink grapefruit juice,
> eat beets and spinach, close my office door to relax midday.
> How amusing, a whole-health spirit guide!

Madi Nolan, doctor of Tibetan medicine and ordained Tibetan lama, offered a past-life regression session, and I was eager to attend. The ferry ride to her island home was peaceful, as a vibrant orange sunrise awoke the eastern horizon. Wild sweet peas, so pretty in pink, lined her street in cheerful greeting. The intention was to regress to lifetimes that held our core issue. I wondered: *Why is food such a dominant factor in my life? Why does my stomach always want to feel stuffed? And why does this consume so much of my attention?*

Those attending had previous experience with past lives and responded easily to the hypnotic induction. Together we breathed deeply going down... down... down... into subconscious terrain. Immediately, a samurai warrior appeared to me, sitting cross-legged with a sword stuck in his gut. I simply noticed.

We went down, down, down to another lifetime. I stopped to look around. I was barefoot, a young girl in a hut, wearing a soiled gunnysack dress; my brothers and sisters were lined up sleeping on a mattress; and my beloved collie (from this life's childhood) was at my side. This lifetime was during the Irish potato famine and we were starving! Emotions rose up, tears fell. This felt real! I thought about "mother's milk," an image that had come to mind a couple of weeks earlier as I was eating sweets in this lifetime. Milk in this Irish scene came from goat, but there was no goat. I offered the girl a bowl of milk; she offered me a green shamrock.

We breathed even more deeply into the next past life, going way, way down into what felt like the bowels of earth. A deep vibrational tone rippled, reminding me of Gyuto Monks' tantric chants, known for their "otherworldly" sound. Now a dinosaur, I munched yummy green plants in a lush rain forest. This evoked a feeling of love for this ancient reptile and prehistoric time on earth.

We then traveled to our "parallel universe."

> *Recent discoveries in quantum physics (the study of the physics of sub-atomic particles) and in cosmology (the branch of astronomy and astrophysics that deals with the universe taken as a whole) shed new light on how mind interacts with matter. These discoveries compel acceptance of the idea that there is far more than just one universe and that we constantly interact with many of these "hidden"* [parallel] *universes.*
> —www.manyuniverses.com

Yellow sun appeared round like a medicine wheel with nourishing "nipples" around the rim. I pressed my hand against the nipples and felt pulsating force—a true source of nourishment. I then saw Mother Earth with nipples or portals with energetic "milk" pouring forth.

After the emotional regression, we came back to the here and now and stood on a medicine wheel that Madi had prepared. We were instructed to walk clockwise and sense when to stop on the wheel. I spontaneously stopped in the southwest as Japanese flute music played. Here, in a meditative brainwave state, I took samurai warrior's hands and removed the sword from his gut. An emptying "swoosh" lifted the warrior and I upward, higher and higher… into Light.

These regressions into and impressions from past lives were powerfully alive, merging time and space. Now, I better understood my obsession with food and its mysteries. Now, I could continue my healing path in nourishing sun substance.

A few years ago, I attended a weeklong retreat near Santa Cruz with Michael Meade, a storyteller, author, and scholar of mythology, anthropology, and psychology. Michael's insightful storytelling, passionate drumming and singing grabs you by the soul and transports you to distant tribal cultures. Driving on the mountain road to this event, I looked down into a green ravine and received the impression of a mushroom, and next to it a gnome! A magical retreat started right there, then included rituals in nature, foot-washing rites, dream work, and honest interaction. At this retreat, Michael said, "What is wounded in this world can only be healed in the other world; we are the agents of healing the other world; and healing is a revolutionary act."

As we talked about our personal stories, I learned from Michael that a nickname such as "Fatty Patty" is a curse and that there is a blessing in a curse. The blessing for me was to change my name from Patty to Trish and thus help erase the memory of that timid, self-conscious self.

> Food-frenzy vortex,
> I sit and close my eyes.
> Suddenly, a body separates from me
> with whirlwind force.
> She was the one out of balance.
> Who is she? Ghost? Inner child?
> A lesson in identity.

Trish Blog — Soil and Soul

I received an email from a man. Its sentiment touched me to the core. His words expressed gratitude, hurt, weakness, and pride for the circumstances in his life. This man is not "on the make" looking to get something sexually. He is genuine inside out—a rare gem. This communication brought up hurt feelings and tearful memories of my emotionally unavailable father and the empty space inside.

My body is toxic again with too many sweet/acidic foods. I forget (go unconscious) and resort to unhealthy eating patterns. I appreciate body parts communicating inflammation. I will continue to heal my relationship with food and treat my body with more intelligence.

As I interact with people who are genuine and shine Light, my soul and soil will be nourished at new depth. This personal work transpires with collective work. We heal as one body, which is why it is critical that I/we do my/our inner work. Rays of hope shine. The body's soul and soil give and receive messages that our intention is whole health.

Units of Energy

An inner voice tells me it is not attracted to sweets, overeating, and unavailable men. To my surprise, the thought is not putting me into a reactionary tailspin. Did an old pattern shift as something new opened? I am being imprinted with new information and discover that I have a new capacity to observe the old passing away and the new being born.

My *Aware Eating* (personal coaching and hypnotherapy for women who struggle with food and weight) coach, Robin Maynard-Dobbs, says that I am now vibrating differently and will draw to me relationships that are nourishing. I begin to choose relationships with food, men, and women that vibrate harmoniously. Doing so has an instant effect. I no longer feel alone in this realm, as my life fills up on units of energy (calories) that support overall health.

> We are by nature observers, and thereby learners. That is our permanent state.
>
> —Ralph Waldo Emerson

Chapter 21
Oversoul ~ Blog 2006

I was delighted when I met my inner selves—my spiritual, emotional, mental, and physical bodies. Listening to their individual voices and watching them play their unique roles in my day-to-day life was entertaining, even comical. This chorus line, with a choreographer named Resistance, offered an "individuation" process that integrated my ego personality. They all put on quite a show in these blog posts from 2006.

Cocoon

I asked my household of emotional, mental, and physical bodies if they wanted to go to the river under night sky. Bodies responded, "No, no, no! It's too expansive. We want to be in our cocoon right now." I turned within and asked, "Who is doing this asking? Who is behind these thoughts, feelings, and words? Who is this observer of self? And who is the observer observing the observer?" The answer looped back in one word: "Oversoul."

Who Does She Think She Is?

Who does this Oversoul character think she is, anyway? Coming into our space and taking charge? We bodies have been handling things quite well for years now. Hah! She wants to change things? Nonsense! Why, just this morning she had us held hostage for two hours, determining what we would eat for breakfast. She has this notion that we are a gyroscopic household and that eating habits need to change to sustain pH in an upright position of balance. She wants us to learn when we are tilting into acidic, or "toxic," territory. We were ready to dive into cookie dough, but she put the brakes on that one. Not even one bite! She suggested this "yummy" sprout salad with celery and walnuts, but we went a different direction. A compromise you might say, with a nutritious soup that took two hours to prepare. What's with all her stillness, introspection, and wisdom? Did she come from some monastery? What I want to know is this: "What's for dessert?" Does she really expect me to change my nature? My name, after all, is Resistance, and I expect to live up to it! She does, however, have a way of sweet-talking and getting my attention. She told me, and this household, we could have treats but not in the same way as before. Humph! I still wanna know who she thinks she is!"

Busted

That Oversoul ruined my day! Just when I was getting my way with the favorite gingerbread recipe and bottle of molasses, she turned to me and said, "Busted!" She picked up on the subtle sexual currents and asked the household of emotional, mental, physical bodies why the prospect of eating gingerbread was creating a sensual/sexual response. Our answer: "Food is like sex, giving pleasure and comfort. This chemistry has been part of our environment since we developed in the womb." Oversoul would hear none of it, saying we could have gingerbread when the compulsive behavior stopped. She is really getting on my nerves! Sweets have distracted my household from inner emptiness and we can't let that go! Why change now after all these years? Well, Oversoul seems to think the household can have a different sensuality and sexuality that doesn't focus on sugar. Now what on earth does that look like... and taste like?

Lesson of a Drain Pipe

The sink in our home needs constant attention. We can never get the thing unclogged. Sunday, in the midst of the gingerbread bust, we took the plunger to that sink's drainpipe and, with determination, got something to move. Little by little, bits of black gunk released and globs of the stuff came up. Yuk! What a surprise! We thought the gunk would be pushed through the pipe, but no. It was pulled up by the force of suction.

Oversoul says this is a good example of how consciousness works with its levels of unconscious, subconscious, conscious, and super-conscious. The vibrational pressure of one level has a pulling force on the next level. She says this is not hierarchy, as each level is critical to the next—parts of one circulating support system—just like our household of bodies.

Oversoul has been putting pressure on this household to release old unhealthy patterns. A recent shift in consciousness, she says, allowed her to plunge more fully and thus bring up old childhood patterns into awareness—old patterns that we were quite content with.

We're still not sure about this Oversoul entity, but she is gaining our trust as we begin to experience what an unclogged system feels like. As a household, we watch the water go freely and fully down the drain with a healthy gurgling sound. She has our curiosity piqued as we wonder what's next. But then she reminds us to stay in the *now!*

What on earth is going on when oneness is being compared to a drainpipe? We conclude that Creator must have one heck of a sense of humor, with mirrors everywhere to reflect a lesson. Oversoul says that they're lessons of Truth which include law and order. So is this lesson the law and order of a drainpipe? "Yes," she says.

Fun Adventures

Under wings of Oversoul we finally got out of our cocoon and went to the river. We ended up next to blackberry bushes under a pink, blossoming cherry tree. Two towhees landed as the wind churned up and danced with rain. We all loved it! Later we watched the movie *Peter Pan*. We joined in the chorus. "We do believe in fairies. We do! We do! We do!"

At the flower essence workshop with Camilla Blossom we caught trouble from Oversoul. We were just having fun, and you know what she did? She got our attention and pulled us back in the workshop circle, telling us to stop being distracted, sit still, and listen. Camilla didn't help with that soft grounding voice and meditation that made us receptive and even peaceful.

Camilla invited the workshop participants to make an aromatherapy potion full of flower power. With Oversoul guiding we mixed lavender (soothing, moves stuck energy, relaxing), geranium (balances hormones, moods, skin, and heart, opens doors for receiving), and eucalyptus (releases old structures, beliefs, habits, patterns, and disperses negative energy). Mental body added grapefruit (purification, good for overeating issues, releases mental chatter, cleanses aura of denser energies), and rose (unconditional love human and divine, heals emotional wounds, heart and liver tonic/strengthener, self-love). Physical body chose ylang-ylang (sensual acceptance, release of inhibitions, calming, integrating, healing abandonment issues). Camilla asked us to name our potion. Telling the workshop circle about our name change from Patty, as in "Fatty Patty," to Trish, we got it! Our flower essence potion name is "Trish." So now Oversoul wants the household to wear this flower essence. As Resistance, I see that our old unhealthy patterns are doomed!

And this morning, we flew in a dream. All the household bodies were conscious and sitting together on an energetic force field, traveling above the countryside. We kept exclaiming, "This is the physical dimension, and we are flying above it!" We flew high, low, and in-between trees. It was so fun flying free, just like Peter Pan!

Earth Wave

It wasn't an earthquake but an earthwave. Household of bodies felt it move and we listened, watched, and rode the strong waves. As the house creaked, we considered getting up and dressed to prepare for the effects of the waves. Looks like we went back to sleep, since here it is morning and we are in the same plane of existence, seemingly unchanged. Somewhere, however, something major shifted! It was impressive in its powerful waving vibration. Maybe elementals of a new nature were moving into alignment. Whatever their nature, be they subtle or dense, these forces have my deepest respect.

Mother Types

"Logic does not float this boat" rang through our household at 3:30 a.m. It reminded us of the "earth wave" currents we felt yesterday and of flying through space. All senses say there has been a shifting of gears.

Oversoul was happy yesterday. I, Resistance, was not. We went to the bank that was in a grocery store and we all wanted a treat. Did we get that? No! Oversoul said, "You can wait." And no one, absolutely no one, in this entire household put up a fuss! There was not even a hint of back-talk static! Now how can I live up to my reputation when no one will work with me, Resistance? I told that Oversoul character that I was going to leave and find a new household. She asked me to stay and suggested there might be a new role for me, something very important that only I can fulfill. I told her I would wait and see. She said we would do that together. Humph! These mother types!

Voice of Ancestors

Standing next to cottonwood and poplar trees, we saw a long straight branch. We had been thinking about fence posts for our circle garden and now envisioned this branch as a "medicine pole" grounded in the center, with attached feathers, chimes, and beads. We walked to the branch and picked it up to take home. We stopped, however, as a feeling-thought-image came in. "People on the walking trail are going to think we're weird. Wait! People already think we're weird… this will simply add to it." We put the branch back on the ground and stood still. Picking it up again, we started home. Then we heard an inner voice say, "Nothing has or will stop creativity and imagination from flowing. It is inner nature."

Underworld Tears

This household was wide awake from 3:00 to 7:00 a.m., noticing that our landscape had changed, the internal pressure cooker had subsided, and the emotional roller coaster was still. We were in a bright, quiet, tranquil plateau. After falling asleep, we awoke crying. In our dreams, we were processing grief, assisting others in processing grief, and mourning a death. This household cannot get away from grief. We are all connected underground like the community of nettle we clipped for soup, the self-heal creeping along in purplish hue, and the cleavers climbing outside our door. We are connected above ground in light and below ground in grief.

Labyrinth Dance

This household of feeling, thought, and action dances an emotional spectrum. In sunny weather, we are joyous and outgoing; in dark weather, we are sad and depressed. When high, a voice says, "Be aware, you are about to dive into sadness." And when low, a voice says, "Be aware, you are about to rise into new heights." Is Oversoul the one speaking in this household of changing weather patterns?

My household of bodies asks why we have to go through this constant motion of being churned in currents and slammed against the shore again and again. The answer is simple: dancing in creative process with dynamic e-motional forces is what we came here to learn. This earth dance of turn and return is a loving labyrinth of self-discovery.

Inner Marriage

Emotional, mental, and physical bodies join in partnership and commit to communicating openly through thick and thin. This inner marriage expands in trust and blooms with passion. Marriage between two people is not based on "'til death do we part." It is based on unconditional love that supports spiritual development within oneself, with one's partner, and in the relationship. Without spiritual substance, marriage dies. As we write, we hear Oversoul saying she wants our household to be happy and fulfilled. She is pulling for all of us to be more enlightened in our relationships. There's that plunger again with its suction effect—pulling light through matter.

> Teaching is an instinctual art, mindful of potential,
> craving of realizations, a pausing, seamless process.
>
> —A. Bartlett Giamatti

Chapter 22
Seamless Reality ~ A Teaching

I wrote this "teaching" early on my spiritual journey. It was inspired by angry people working for peace and spiritual people who were not walking their talk. There appeared to be two realities, one fragmented with seams and the other intact and seamless.

Look around. What do you see? Is it a world that is coming apart at the seams? A world overpopulated, overdrugged, overweight, overmaterialistic, overindulgent, oversexed, overdeveloped, and overpolluted? Look inside. What do you feel? Is it a world that is coming apart at the seams? An inner world that is fearful, depressed, anxious, stressed, unhappy, and confused? Do both worlds feel like a tangled maze, trapping you with no way through and no way out?

There is a way through and a way out. The starting point is within reach and one need not travel any distance, lose ten pounds, own an expensive home, or get a college degree to find it. The starting point is within one's personal field of awareness.

When we are ready, and if we are willing, we can identify threads that bind us and keep us in an imbalanced and unhappy state. And though negative patterns of thinking and limiting habits of behavior are deeply enmeshed, we can, with intention, identify them, pull on them, and eventually release them. It's not an easy process. It's not a comfortable journey. As one pulls on threads holding distorted patterns, memories of personal grief and loss come into awareness. It's not easy to realize that *yes—I did lose parts of myself in childhood and in relationships. And yes, I continue to act in ways that are not supporting my well-being.* As we loosen and release tangled inner threads and find new clarity, we join the growing numbers of others doing the same. Individual healing leads to collective healing.

Seamed reality, based in separation and divisiveness, is sewn with threads of opinions and choices based in self-centeredness. It thrives on a "me vs. you" and "us vs. them" mentality. The patterns of this seamed fabric are separation of left and right brain, logic and feeling, mind and heart, and matter and spirit, extending as separation between humans and nature, men and women, and cultures and countries. These threads have been woven for so long that we have forgotten the seamless reality that unifies through heart-centeredness of Love.

There is plenty of support to keep us in destructive patterns individually and collectively. One doesn't need to look far; mainstream media will be the first with the "news." Seamless reality suggests taking personal *response*-ability for one's own internal chaos and the chaos in the world. This is not for passive and silent types but for planetary warriors who wage transformative action and lead the way.

How does one untangle toxic threads and begin a healing process? Turning within to listen deeply is a good first step. Listening can lead one to realize it is time to let go of a job, a relationship, unhealthy eating habits, or lifestyle. Listening that could mean change. How many are willing to let go of the old to make room for the new?

As threads of chaos disintegrate, new threads integrate. What do threads of order look like? Each of us has our own story to tell, our own fabric to weave. Threads that filled the void when my life unraveled were meditation, an angel, jogging, nature, and church. What threads pull at your heartstrings and weave you in well-being? What threads lift your spirit? Once these positive threads are identified, given focus, and supported, they will guide the way.

Weaving new identity and reality is not for the weak-hearted. Within tangled threads are toxic demons to face, wrestle, and release. As a collective body of people living a mythic journey, we have an incredible opportunity to weave a new planetary story for ourselves and for Gaia.

There is no place I go that is not faery realm. My kin are everywhere.

—David Spangler, The Lorian Foundation

Chapter 23
Dosewallips ~ A Story

The Dosewallips State Park, in Washington State, is one of my favorite rainforest destinations. I frequently visit to attune with the elements and to express gratitude. I captured one visit with this story.

In the moment of now (never long ago, or far away), a young-at-heart miss steps into the welcoming green arms of the Olympic Rainforest at a place of enchantment called Dosewallips. The wet, wild nature of this temperate lowland forest quenches her soul. Vibrant chartreuse moss dripping from old growth trees, Douglas fir and western hemlock, quenches her pores.

Driving by car to the trailhead, she witnesses, by the side of the road, a face of significant character and strength. It is weather carved in stone with tufts of grass as hair. "Stop the car! Back up!" she exclaims to the one and only passenger—herself. And yes, there he is! A warrior and shaman with buffalo look. How long has he been here keeping watch? Have others seen and honored this guardian of the Dosewallips? She sees and she honors.

At the trailhead, the colors and textures of the changing season nourish her senses: ancient evergreen tree branching against golden maple, creating a protective canopy; spongy moss radiating green in all directions, inviting her quiet step; overturned decaying stump with roots exposed and vines entangled, creating a sci-fi work of art; and laughing waterfall, providing background music to this day of leisure. Surely, this is home and here, her very own living room!

Walking the trail, she raises her arms, acknowledging the spirit world pressing in around her from east, south, west, and north. "I know you. I enter in consciousness," she announces. Her lifeblood pulsates as she breathes harmoniously with this natural world.

Sitting on a bridge, eating a bran muffin, she hears a voice say, "You need not eat. Going hungry sharpens the senses." "Thank you," her natural response, is greeted by a "thank-you" in return. This familiar exchange never fails to delight her.

She rests at the campground, with her back against a rock, beside the Dosewallips River. Trees, plants, soil, rock, and water spring to life, dancing and singing, as if an animated Walt Disney movie. Her attention shifts to the Dosewallips River, where she now sits with river rock friends around her. One or two always nudge her, asking to be taken home to her windowsill. It takes only a minute for her to locate the right pair, smooth and grey: the round one, representing the womb of female; the elongated one, representing the phallus of male. She knows the power of these fertility symbols in a barren world. Her "energy work" is to bring these female and male forces back to life, assisting in the healing of her beloved planet, Gaia. Her task is to honor and nourish greening forces that give birth to the power of spiritual Love.

She hears voices call, "Come and rest in my lavish ferns under cedar, fir, and hemlock. Come, yield in the cradle of fairy country." If only she could stay to sing and dance with her friends as they reveled in the turning seasons of Dosewallips. But stay she could not. Her home was the city with responsibilities in the "real" world. She came away, however, with senses full, having absorbed all that she could in one day.

After returning to the city, she learned the meaning of Dosewallips.

> "The name Dosewallips comes from a Twana Indian myth about a man named Dos-wail-opsh who was turned into a mountain at the river's source."
> —en.wikipedia.org/wiki/Dosewallips_River

She had met this one in his place of mystical power. May he live! May wilderness live!

> In sacred places, the spiritual and the physical are experienced together. Sacred places are openings between the heavens and the earth, or between the surface of the earth and the underworld; they are places where different planes or levels of experience cross.
>
> —Rupert Sheldrake, *The Rebirthing of Nature*

Chapter 24
Sacred Sites ~ Sacred Times

There are places in nature that sing to us, welcoming us home. There are times of year honoring Earth and Sun, turning and returning. Sacred sites and sacred times fill us with reverence.

Sacred Natural Sites: An Overview, (www.sacredland.org/home/resources/tools-for-action/protection-strategies-for-sacred-sites/what-is-a-sacred-site/#sthash.MfNCeytW.dpuf), reported by Anthony Thorley and Cecilia M. Gunn in 2008, gave "sacred site" an operational definition so that it could be easily recognized by many cultures and groups and be part of international discussion and recognition: "A sacred site is a place in the landscape, occasionally over or under water, which is especially revered by a people, culture or cultural group as a focus for spiritual belief and practice and likely religious observation."

An "operational definition" does not tell me when I am at a sacred site. My body tells me through its parts: feet rooted, hands tingling, senses sharpened, head light, and heart resonating. And Spirit tells me through my whole being: a "sacred site" is the presence of peace and power, where nature and cosmic energy merge as one reverberating grid.

Road trips take me through my Pacific Cascadia bioregion where I stop to attune with sacred sites.

Dash Point Park

Setting sun kissing Olympic peaks,
hypnotic power with words to speak
of solar beings observing too,
this sun in motion one with you.

Ti' Swaq Enchantment

Shallow breathing in the city,
telephone lines netting me in.
Let me out, get me away,
to wide-open places, and wild green spaces.
Tahoma Peak calling, and the stars,
I must be close to the stars.
Ti' Swaq sensually curved,
Tahoma ruggedly peaked.
I sketch their lines kissing sky,
where spirit and matter meet.

Vision quests are often experienced at sacred sites. These rites of passage are filled with purpose.

Sedona

Here not to seek
but to create a link,
honoring this place

in the cosmos,
so a page can turn
and a new story be told.
Sun shines on red rock.
I shine in response.

Banff

Bow Falls' rock throne:
mossy seat inviting,
waterfall laughing,
sage smoke prayerful.
Stillness,
vision quest within.

Solstice and equinox ceremonies allow us to celebrate Earth's love affair with Sun. This celestial turning of Matter and Light is a sacred sight.

Golden Gardens Park

Equinox water blessing
weaving time and timelessness.
Smudge smoke cleansing, clearing.
Fire circle containing, warming.
Bodies drumming, chanting.
Water shimmering, shape-shifting.
Dragon-mouth cloud,
swallows Olympic peaks.

Grove of the Patriarchs

Held between grandmother cedars
deep chants rise from the bowels of earth.
Silenced when people walk by.

A sacred site is anywhere, anytime one is conscious of connecting to something larger than oneself.

Skagit Valley

Yellow tulip sunbursts,
a gift from soil to vase
adding movement and sound
to this living room.

Las Vegas

Neon ooze above clinking machines,
people dazed by glitz, glitter
and the almighty dollar.
Give me moon, sun,
and wide open space
of Cascade Mountains
emitting power and grace.

> If such a consciousness truly is set loose in the world, nothing will be the same. It will free us to be in a sacred body, on a sacred planet, in sacred communion with all of it. It will infect the universe with holiness.
>
> —Sue Monk Kidd, *The Dance of the Dissident Daughter*

Chapter 25
Goddess Flesh ~ A Prayer

Goddess was a powerful force early in my spiritual journey. She made me feel alive, as if She lived and breathed through me. Her elements were my elements and I came to know my own nature as Earth, Water, Air, and Fire.

This flesh is Goddess flesh. This earth is Goddess earth. We share miles and miles of terrain, brought to life by invisible grids of energy. We share patterns and pathways sacred.

Energy vortexes of dancing light coil from crown to root and root to crown as Kundalini Serpent sets matter afire. Ignited glands—ovaries, adrenals, pancreas, heart, thyroid, pituitary and pineal circulate vital life force, generating core substance of who I am—creating my personal environment.

Pollutants of body—be gone! Pollutants of mind—be gone! Pollutants of heart—be gone! Let my fire burn clean and bright.

This flesh is Goddess flesh. This earth is Goddess earth. We share miles and miles of terrain, brought to life by invisible grids of energy. We share patterns and pathways sacred.

Energy vortexes of dancing light spiral from sun to earth and earth to sun as Kundalini Serpent sets matter afire. Ignited pathways—Stonehenge, Dragon Hill, Machu Picchu, Ayers Rock, the Great Pyramid, Grand Canyon, and Mt. Baker (Sleeping Dragon) emit vital life force, generating core substance of who She is—creating Her global environment.

Pollutants of earth—be gone! Pollutants of air—be gone! Pollutants of water—be gone! Let Her fire burn clean and bright.

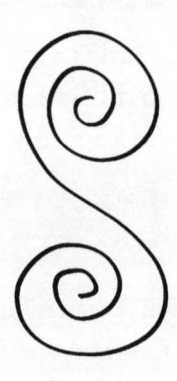

> The mandala is an archetypal image whose occurrence is attested throughout the ages. It signifies the wholeness of the Self. This circular image represents the wholeness of the psychic ground or, to put it in mythic terms, the divinity incarnate in [hu]man.
>
> —Carl Jung, *Memories, Dreams, and Reflections*

CHAPTER 26
CIRCLE OF LIFE

The circle of life acquired new meaning when my mother passed over, from flesh to spirit. One door closed, another opened and Mom was still part of it all—from the other side.

One day at Mom's assisted living facility, I saw that she was in pain, with redness in her foot spreading up her leg. Alarmed, I insisted that she go to the hospital. That night at her bedside, we talked heart-to-heart. She confided that, after eighty-five years, her spiritual values were closest to those of Native Americans because of their respect for nature. She knew how much I loved nature and her statement bonded us in a new way. Mom wrote her grocery list and I agreed to bring the items in a couple of days, when she was back at the care facility. Leaving the hospital, I remembered hearing her nurse use the term "amputation." At age eighty-five, with her weak heart, I knew that was not going to happen. I also remembered hearing Mom say, for the first time, "If I make it to age eighty-six."

The next day, Mom thanked me for insisting that she be hospitalized, but when I saw her on life support, I questioned my action. If I had left her in the care facility, she wouldn't be on life support now. Why did I feel so strongly about her being at the hospital? I didn't even like hospitals with their machines and medications. A niece gave me the answer, saying it gave family time to gather around her the way she would have wanted. And so it was. One by one, siblings and other family members packed into Mom's hospital room and huddled around her bed. We witnessed her heart stabilize, and even pick up pace when family members hugged her. Mom was strong in spirit; her body was far from strong. Family agreed to take her off life support at nine in the morning, January 4, 2008. Hand in hand, each one expressed their love and let her go. This solidarity of Mom's large tribe brought tears to the eyes of the hospital chaplain.

Trish Blog, 2007 and 2008

Finger Rays

A man who lies to himself, me, and others came to mind. He is in deep. The other night, he asked how to get out. I told him thread by thread. The problem is he can't even begin, due to dishonesty. As a result, he keeps asking the same question and going nowhere. Then I thought to send him white Light. The Light didn't manifest through mind's-eye-imaging. This time it came through my fingers and thumb! I moved my finger "rays" around to see how it felt. It was like having long fingernails. I envisioned this man in the midst of my finger web of light, reminding me of Spider-Man, the current hero of my grandson, Parker.

Soul Sisters

Driving to the hospital, there was a moment when I sensed something lift skyward. It was Mom, and these words appeared in my mind's eye: "soul sisters." A little later, thinking about family, I sensed a host of angels gathering around. I shared that story with family members and someone asked to speak to me privately, suggesting that sometimes I say too much, that others need time to process in their own way. I responded that I can only be spontaneous, from my heart. Receiving this criticism, I retreated into my inner world where I feel understood and safe. In my outer world, I feel like an alien—even more so now that I have ET fingers!

When I told a brother-in-law about Mom feeling close to nature, he suggested a Native American ceremony at her burial site. He suggested I find a shaman to offer the eulogy. I called two Native American friends, asking if they would be available to offer prayer at Mom's funeral. Both said, "Trish, you can do that!" Gulp! Could I be that open in public about my spiritual path, about my deepest feelings? Could I use my medicine drum and speak in honor of my mother? Yes, I could, and after getting positive feedback from my family, I did.

Cutting four-inch squares of Mom's favorite Hawaiian pink cotton dress, I made spirit bundles to give to family members. In the bundles, I placed feather for air, rock for earth, ash for fire, shell for water, a red bead from one of her necklaces for earth and sky, and fir tree needles for green heart. When I thought about Mom's life and what I might say, I found myself organizing her life in a circle with east as childhood, south as adolescence, west as adulthood, and north as elderhood. This circular pattern is how natural cycles move, from sunrise and spring, to noon and summer, to sunset and autumn, and to night and winter. At the funeral, I honored Mom's circle of life, and with drum in hand I found myself spontaneously singing an earth chant. The chant, written and sung by Denean, a singer, songwriter and recording artist, is always with me, and plays me when it chooses.

Song To The Mother

I walk your sacred ground.
Healing waters I have found.
Rivers flowing strong and deep,
wash away your tears.
Mother, I hear your cry.
I feel your every sigh.
I have come to comfort you.
Around the medicine wheel.
—www.denean.com/documents/221.html

Mom raised her family in Puyallup. A family member brought red cedar from the Puyallup Indian Reservation. The cedar smoke cleansed and purified the site. Offering the ceremony, I felt my legs and feet ground, heart soar, and body reverberate. I shed fear and doubt, offering "spirit medicine" with my blood family. This was the first time I had expressed myself in public as a medicine woman, and I was not the same. Nothing was the same.

Trish Blog, 2008

Thinning Veil

Alone today I felt Mom's cheek against mine, our hands touching in the way we used to say good-bye. I never knew how much love moved between us until she passed over the veil—the veil that now thins.

Pink Nails in Heaven

I thought about Mom today. I no longer drive south to visit her. Now I visit her whenever one of us reaches out for the other. Now I feel her and communicate spiritually.

She is no longer in need of groceries, clothing, or having her nails painted bright pink. I'm happy that she went into Spirit realm with bright pink nails. And though this brings up tears, there is a comforting knowing that she is near, in the same way she was near when she held me on her lap reading nursery rhymes. This morning my body acted on impulse and I found myself asking, "Why am I walking toward the drawer for matches?" The response: "A candle for Mom." I placed a candle on the altar with her picture, spirit bundle, and bright floral material from her favorite dress.

Mom's passing and telling her circle of life story inspired me to write *Turtle's Circle of Life*, a creation story about Turtle's relationship with the four directions and her transformation into Turtle Island. When I discovered I was going to Kona, Hawaii, for my niece's wedding, I designed a *Circle of Life —Mapping One's Story* activity booklet and class to share with students at TuTu's House, a community health and wellness resource center in Kamuela, Hawaii.

When I returned home to the mainland, I reached out to Native American tribes, senior centers, and retirement facilities. I found few non-native seniors eager to sign up for storytelling and mandala art. Why is art and telling one's story a lost art? Are people unaware of the precious gems that make up the chapters of their lives? Or is this feminine inside-out activity too unfamiliar? I did discover, however, that Native people at longhouses, community centers, elder programs, youth clubs, and powwows were receptive to telling their circle of life stories and creating mandalas. Native, indigenous people relate to the circle of life. It is, after all, their way of living—and being.

Circles

> Everything an Indian does is in a circle, and that is because the
> Power of the World always works in circles
> and everything tries to be round.
> The sky is round and the earth is round
> like a ball and so are all the stars.
> —Black Elk, *Black Elk Speaks*

Painful wounds from childhood prevented some attendees from participating in circle mapping, making colorful mandalas of their life stories. They were shut down emotionally and artistically, not wanting to remember.

At the Duwamish Longhouse, one teenage girl sat motionless for fifteen minutes, unable to start her map. Slowly, she began the process. Skipping east of childhood, she went directly to the south, sketching a few images, and then, in west, she increased the fluidity of lines as she added colors. She filled in North with bold and clear images telling her current story of hope and gratitude. Her dark childhood drama and the energy around it was transformed on paper. This teenage girl's resilience in life was reflected in her circle of life map. One thirteen-year-old boy drew a picture of Mount McKinley, in the east of infancy, a basketball in the south of early childhood, weight-lifting in the west of late childhood, and a canoe in the north of current time, representing the canoe journey that his culture celebrated annually. Circle mandalas are as diverse in expression and form as snowflakes, and just as beautiful.

The United Indian Seattle Seafair Days Pow Wow, at Daybreak Star Indian Cultural Center, was a fitting venue for circle of life mapping. One man who had read the activity book said, "A lot of thinking went into the book." I countered his statement with, "A lot of living went into the book." I was amazed at the variety of ways people related to circle mapping. One woman's sister was dying from brain tumors and she needed a tool to help her manage grief and tell her sister's story; another woman considered circle mapping for a family reunion since her mom, at age ninety, had written a story about turtle; another woman was interested in being trained to teach circle mapping to others. A lot of energy and smiles bounced back, forth, and around. We were creating our own colorful circle of life—a living mandala. The highlight of the activity for me was acknowledging and honoring the uniqueness of each student's completed map and telling them that their story was special—one of a kind. Men often filled in their circle maps with words regarding where they had been and what they did; women filled in the space with more colors and symbols. A friend, who is an artist, drew a red swing set in the east of her map. When she completed her map and told her story, an "ah-ha" realization sparked for her: the swing set in the east had the design AA, and in the west of her life, she attended AA. She wondered if this meant that she was predestined to be in AA.

The healing power of circle/mandala art flows, when we open to it, through our unconscious, subconscious, and conscious minds. At times we are fortunate to witness these different levels of the psyche speak as one coordinated and fluid voice. When people mapped their circle of life and told their stories, free-flowing, childlike expressions replaced blocks of fear.

I have met many wonderful elders, adults, and youth in my circle of life classes in Washington State. I was quite surprised the day I taught elders at the Yakama Tribe in eastern Washington and a woman signed her mandala map, "Great-great-granddaughter of Chief Joseph." It was, and continues to be, an honor to meet people who are willing to share their life stories through circle mapping.

As I work with circles through mandala art and storytelling, I connect with a rich history. The oldest known dances were circular, symbolizing the cyclical nature of life. Sacred sites and vortexes were marked by circles of stone. Round drums were used around fires, in ceremonies and in ritual ceremony that mirrored the inner journey to one's center of Self. Healing rites took place within the protection of a sacred circle. The circle is an ancient celestial song that sings through us if we step in and participate, singing along.

> The changing of Bodies into Light, and Light into
> Bodies, is very conformable to the Course of Nature,
> which seems delighted with transmutations.
>
> —Sir Isaac Newton

Chapter 27

Winged Flight

Wings have played a central role in my mystical journey. In ordinary and non-ordinary states of consciousness, wings have given my life exhilaration and spiritual dimension. Jonathan Livingston Seagull showed me how to soar above the flock and Archangel Michael impressed me with feathers of white. I discovered that I, too, had wings!

My intuitive Sacred Feminine was dominant at the beginning of my spiritual journey. I followed Her feelings, dreams, intuition, and visions into right-brain territory and mirrored Her way of seeing and being. Gradually I noticed another presence, my logical Sacred Masculine, giving Her helpful feedback and boundaries. As I watched and listened to this interaction I found She and He increasingly turning toward one another. What was unique about their relationship? What was the generative power between them? Honesty! There was nothing that could get past them without conscious review. They caught every drama, wrong turn in the road, and stuck pattern of behavior, and, once caught, they examined the situation…together…intuitively and logically. This internal care-taking (Love) supported the highest in each other and created vibrational harmony that circulated throughout my whole body.

As a result of this unified combustion I felt heat and tingling across my upper back, between my shoulder blades. What caused these East/West ripples? Was I inflamed from eating too many carbohydrates and pH imbalance? What, exactly, was my body telling me? Time passed. I watched, I listened and then I understood. The tingling at my upper back was associated with the increasing communication between She (my right-brain hemisphere), and He (my left-brain hemisphere). At the same time I noticed that my dreams and visions carried East/West themes. What was my body telling me in real time and in dream time?

And then I found the answer! Why had I not heard of this throughout my years of spiritual exploration? Why had I not read this before? Thanks to the Lightworkers blog, (www.lightworkers.org/blog/159567/wing-chakra), the mystery resolved and I was elated!

Finally, the missing puzzle piece: "The wing chakra is an important instrument for the Angel-Human!" Not only was I an angel in a spiritual sense, my subtle and physical body had angel wings! Why had this critical part of our spiritual anatomy been lost, forgotten? My wing chakra had activated, linking my earthly self with my divine Self. Wow! I now had wings to fly! Where would they take me? What would they teach?

> *The pituitary gland holds the positive, masculine charge and the pineal holds a negative, feminine charge. When the masculine and feminine energies meet in the brain it is known as the Mystical Marriage. The Mystical Marriage initiates the birth of our multidimensional consciousness...*
> *...The feminine earth energy merges with the masculine pituitary gland and the feminine pineal gland receives the masculine energy from Spirit. When the two awakened chakras' essences meet in the third ventricle, there is the union and harmony of spirit into matter as the*

> *multidimensional forces of spiritual light merge with the matter of our third dimensional brain.*
> —www.revelationarchives.blogspot.com/2013/03/the-third-eye-pineal-and-pituitary.html

Where does the Wing Chakra fit on the chakra system that I outlined in chapter 4? I associate its location with the throat, since communication was such a critical part of its activation. Therefore I place it as number six, after the Throat Chakra:

> Sixth chakra. The WHITE wing chakra represents our ability to transcend the material world and journey to multidimensions. It is located at the upper middle back between the shoulder blades and is associated with the pituitary and pineal glands in the endocrine system.

Thanks to wings, mystical flights into multidimensions exhilarate me. No wings, no lift, and no glide. Wings have played a central role in my S/He Dragon journey and are one of my archetypal symbols. What is an archetype? According to Caroline Myss, in her book *Archetypes: Who Are You?* (Hay House, Inc. /1993), one aspect is that they "originate in our cosmic intelligence." Archangel Michael came into my first meditation with an image of white wings; salamander of my dreamtime evolved into dragon with wings; and now honest interaction between my inner feminine and masculine gave me chakra wings of flight! Each human being has a set of spiritual wings—it is our divine birthright. Humans are fallen angels until we discover and activate our spiritual wings that fly us into higher levels of consciousness and multiple universes.

Flying in one's dreams is such a thrill—exhilarating and mysterious.

This flying dream is from September, 1992.

I flew in my dream last night, sitting on a green balloon. I flew over mountain and meadow. A sweet, tranquil sensation moving with the wind. Thoughts appeared, saying, "This flimsy balloon will never hold. It will burst any minute. It cannot sustain the trip." I relaxed and kept moving. Upon landing, I was greeted by elders who called me "Joseph."

What did the name Joseph signify? I referred to *The Woman's Dictionary of Symbols and Sacred Objects*, (Harper&Row/1988), and read that the Christian legend of Joseph's "rod" (symbolic of phallus), said he was chosen to be Mary's husband, out of a group of suitors, by a symbolic test of fertility. "When all candidates laid their rods on the altar, only Joseph's budded and bloomed... The sacred dove of the Goddess came down from heaven and perched on it," signifying that the Goddess accepted him. This dream was introducing my inner Sacred Masculine, whom I would meet at a conscious level years later.

A flying dream, November 1992:

> I am at the edge of an abyss, a waterfall. I knew I had to step into this empty space and did. Waves of substance poured down over my head with a charged, soothing sensation. To my surprise, I was able to breathe through the downpour.

A flying dream, December 1992:

> I put a band with a green balloon on my head. I flew upward into a tree and house with people. One mother thought I was a bad influence on her children. I put the balloon on again. It is flimsy, yet I have no doubt that it will sustain and carry me. I flew over snow and water fields. It felt buoyant and light—freeing!

A flying dream, October 2004:

> Walking through an area was cumbersome and time consuming, so I flew! I flew through matter! I watched as two frames emerged, one left, one right. I looked more closely to see the difference. The views were one and the same except for a lapse/difference in scenery as if timing was different. I flew by three clocks.

I have not analyzed the repetitive symbols in these dreams, such as the color "green" and "balloon." Being right-brained and intuitive, I am not interested in the dissection of parts. I experience the whole and fuse the parts from an instinctual perspective. However, as I write in this moment, I reflect for myself and my readers: Green is the color of heart chakra, representing the fertility of love. Balloon represents buoyancy of spirit through humility and simplicity. The interpretation of dreams, their meaning and significance, does not involve flexing mental muscle. Dreams are personal windows into soulful living.

Real-time flights, in the form of skydiving, are also exhilarating. Not only did I dive out of a Cessna 182 once, but I also went back a second time. This wasn't my idea. My boyfriend wanted to overcome his fear of heights. We attended two training sessions and boarded a small plane at the Snohomish Air Field. I felt terrified but worked to stay calm emotionally in order to functional physically. At 12,000 feet, it was our turn to dive—solo! My boyfriend went first and, gulp, I was next.

It was challenging to exit the plane, the air pressure so intense. Once out the door, instructions were to hang on the wing strut momentarily while looking sideways into the cockpit for a camera snapshot. "You've got to be kidding!" I thought, fearing I wasn't strong enough to hang on. I didn't hang around, proven by my pale face in the photo as hands released. The caption could have read, "Get me out of here!"

Fear gave way to excitement as I free fell through space with my arms and legs in the appropriate X formation. This letting go and flying free was exciting. I counted "one thousand one, one thousand two, and one thousand three" as instructed to prevent "sensory overload." I then pulled the parachute cord and listened on the headphones for further instructions. Down, down, down I floated while enjoying the expansive view. I wanted more action, however, like theme park rides that tickle the stomach. The instructor told me when to brake, it was up to me to land on my feet—a feat not that easy, I discovered. Hitting the ground with such sudden impact requires coordinated skill and though I had that, I lacked confidence. I injured my knee the second dive so we ended that recreational sport.

I have a friend who once lived in Mexico. She told me that every year monarch butterflies swarmed their property, allowing her to get a close look at caterpillars turning into butterflies. According to her eyewitness account, caterpillars would catch the tips of their tails on the twig of a tree, hang there until their heads fell off, and then turn to mush! This was not the gentle process of furry caterpillar crawling into a cozy chrysalis to be transformed into a beautiful butterfly. This process of dismemberment and dissolution was anything but gentle and cozy. It was intense!

When I heard her story, I realized this was exactly what had happened to me so many years ago. The Kundalini snap at the back of my neck was like losing my head and "mush" is how my brain-body felt for many years. To develop wings and fly, one must be willing to be dismembered in the dark cocoon of the unconscious and do inner work with the still focus of a caterpillar. As rays of light penetrate the cocoon, turning matter to mush, a new form is created. That form, that being, introduced itself to me as S/He Dragon.

S/He Dragon

Shamanic Journey

Mind still, inner eye focused, I look, I see
shoulder blade arms winging left and right.
I am wings, opening to wind's force.
I am not on a flying dragon—I am dragon!
Ahead, I see the arc of earth outlined in space.
I fly toward her dark night with… skyscrapers.
Electromagnetic particles rain down.
What is this? Fairy dust radiation?
Dragon fire?
Am I one with comet, meteorite, or space ship?
Then… sudden turning, a rotation in space.
Dragon rolls with it, flying strong,
shoulder blade arms winging left and right.

> The fluttering of a butterfly's wings can effect climate changes on the other side of the planet.
>
> —Paul Erlich

Chapter 28
Caterpillar to Butterfly ~ A Journey

My experience of wings, flying and transformation called in the butterfly who spoke through this poem.

On the flutter of butterfly wings
I incarnate and engage
in a journey of growth
and process of ascension.

Along the way I feel the flutter
of butterfly wings in a sunset,
a warm face, a kind word.
Yet I return to caterpillar existence
and caterpillar ways.

I am compelled to keep moving.
I let go
yielding to an internal call.

Dark chrysalis holds me, evolves me.

S/He Dragon

I wait as I listen. I listen as I wait.
Stretching, I learn truth. Stretching, I learn love,
from a deep part of myself.

Internal work done, moment is delivered… and I fly!
Soaring heights, seeing more, being more
on wings of consciousness.

> Getting back in touch with our sacred longings entails a spiritual quest – a kind of ecomystical renewal—that can transform our desire, enliven our communities, simplify our lifestyles, and ultimately rekindle our global prospects.
>
> —Mary C. Grey, *Sacred Longings: Ecofeminist Theology and Globalization*

CHAPTER 29

ACHIEVING AND BEING

A sudden change in one's circumstances can be seen as a crisis or an opportunity, depending on one's focus. Clearing the lens to sustain focus is the ongoing task of consciousness. A major shift in my life was about to present itself. Yet, instead of wobbling in crisis I calmly accepted the change. I attribute this to a stable core supported by two brain hemispheres of intuition and logic, wings that kept me aloft, and a loving universe that had supported me all my life.

While walking down the hallway at work, looking out the windows, I realized I didn't want to be there anymore. I sensed something was going to shift—the economic downturn of 2008 set this shift into motion. After eighteen years at the same nonprofit organization, I was joining the ranks of the unemployed, with my new mantra: "Here I grow again."

Ready for new stimulus and opportunities for creativity, I saw this change as an evolutionary leap. When circumstances and relationships reach capacity, change is natural, providing additional space for us to learn new lessons about ourselves, others, and life in general. I admit I was a little shaky on the surface, not knowing what the future held regarding that secure paycheck. On the other hand, unemployment sounded okay; I was ready for new horizons. Feeling stable at my core, knowing the significance of the shift, I celebrated this passage as both an ending and a beginning. This inner stability is what my supervisor referred to when he asked, "Why aren't you in a panic like the others, knowing you will be laid off in another month?"

Identity in this world is based on earning an income and being employed. It is how one contributes and survives. I stepped into the world of unemployment as S/He Dragon, conscious of Sacred Feminine intuition and Sacred Masculine logic that gave me a wider view of the horizon. Unemployment benefits would pay me to go back to school. Was there a school for a dragon? It also offered training and business counseling through the Self-Employment Assistance Program (SEAP). Could a mystical dragon qualify? Could dragons have a business and sell their products of magic?

I celebrated this rite of passage by traveling to California to visit my big sister and to attend Dr. Wayne Dyer's Hollywood movie premiere *The Shift: Taking Your Life from Ambition to Meaning*—another mantra for my adventure into the unknown. I was packed and ready to go as rains poured down and rivers rose up in several local counties. Would I be able to get through the valley and to the airport if I waited until morning? I turned the question over to my angels. Immediately, my son called concerned about the flooding, urging me to drive to his house so he could transport me to the airport in the morning. Quite the response from angels via one earth angel!

The thought of driving Los Angeles freeways made me anxious, causing a sensation of heaviness. I decided to change my thinking and suddenly saw a white, etheric substance fill in an LA street grid making the streets new and safe. This image didn't come with conscious intention or effort. When I simply let go of anxiety, something positive (white substance) instantly filled in the empty space. This is the advantage of being connected to a reptilian brain. One receives immediate instinctual support.

At Seattle's SeaTac airport, I sat in the terminal waiting for departure. In a yoga position, I meditated to center myself and relax. Opening my eyes, I looked directly into the eyes of a man walking toward me. Joyfully, we talked about yoga and spirituality. He commented about the way I was "transmitting," saying that my energy was very sensual, asking if I was single. He wanted to touch hands… a lot. This Italian man's round glasses and large, brown eyes reminded me of Gandhi.

Arriving at my sister's house, I noticed a large tree in the back—trees are also family to me. I walked the block taking pictures of the natural world and connecting energetically as the new kid in town. The trees with large trunks liked being seen and having their pictures taken, as if parched for attention. I felt their energy in my energetic body. As I was talking with my sister at breakfast about male and female energies and my need for more logic, she exclaimed, "Goddess is here!" as a spider descended from midair. The last time that had happened, she was in a woman's circle discussing Goddess.

Sitting under one of my sister's orange trees, I sketched, wrote, and meditated. "This is the work I would like to do full time!" I realized. And why not? In *Shift: At the Frontiers of Consciousness* magazine, the article *The Power of the Collective,* (Issue 15/June-August/2007), by John Hagelin emphasizes the healing power of meditation: "Since meditation provides an effective, scientifically proven way to dissolve individual stress, and if society is composed of individuals, then it seems like common sense to use meditation to similarly defuse societal stress. A reduction in crime and stress-related behavior would then be expected to follow." It occurred to me that President Obama was creating green jobs to stimulate the economy. Could meditation be a green job to increase health and reduce crime and violence? Why not pay people to meditate as a whole health service? I began to write a "Green Heart Project" proposal suggesting this plan.

Grandmother moon rose full, held in the arms of a large elm tree. At five the next morning, I felt the "radiant peace" of simply being. In a flash of insight, I realized my new work was to write a book about the Sacred Feminine, using sketches, poetry, visions, dreams, and stories recorded over many years. My Sacred Masculine was kicking into gear to assist with structure and delivery. How fun! But how does one organize all the material? My sister and brother-in-law, both writers, gave me some tips. At the Getty Villa, I checked in with the muse statues. Do I resonate with the muse of "dance" or of "writing"? I connected to creativity, muse to muse.

Hollywood was not what I expected, and I mentioned to my sister that the atmosphere felt festive, like the Western Washington Fair back home. She commented, "It's definitely not the posh sophistication of Beverly Hills." It was bonding to watch the movie *The Shift: Taking Your Life from Ambition to Meaning* with my big sis and to immerse in the buzz of Hollywood with Wayne Dyer and fans. I was living large for a week, and then back to reality with my modest lifestyle, more job searches, and hopefully, a lot of writing. Living in a multidimensional universe, one never knows what the moment will bring, let alone the extended future. One stays poised on one's feet, resilient enough to turn when it's time. I like living in "the moment of meaning."

I said good-bye to family and drove south. The warm sun and aqua-blue sea of Encinitas welcomed me as I located my beach bungalow getaway. Sweet wind currents, blowing in from the sea, engendered response: "I need a kite to dance these rhythms!" Standing on a hill with outstretched arms, I lean against the currents. I am that kite!

I was surprised to see the Self-Realization Fellowship Temple that was founded by Paramahansa Yogananda in 1920 on a cliff above the beach. A left-brained traveler would have researched tourist sites and been aware of this focal point. Being right-brained and spontaneous, I get to be surprised. I had "met" Yogananda months earlier at Seattle's East West Bookshop, after teaching a "circle of life—mapping one's story" class. Upon leaving the bookshop I noticed a poster on the wall that said "YOGI." When I focused my attention on it, a blast of energy swooped in and "lifted" my head by the neck like a gust of wind. I walked over to the poster and energetically "met" Paramahansa Yogananda. He is one powerful yogi! I consider Yogananda a cosmic friend and consciously honored him as I strolled his temple and grounds. The scent of sage at Cottonwood Creek Park, my next stop, soothed me. The beach was a freeway with meditators, tai chi dancers, surfers, walkers, and joggers. As dusk settled in and people thinned out, I felt the mystical power of this mighty body of water, the Pacific Ocean.

Sea Dragon

Sunset shifts bright yellow to soft purple-orange,
subtle rays bid good-night,
evening star—wish I may, wish I might.
Tiny birds hover above sand
on sweet scent of wood smoke.
People parade thins out
as skyline reddens in hue.
How vulnerable is this coast?
Very, I would guess.
Then… words appear, instinctually: "Sea Dragon."
Then… mystical particles wash over me.
Then… I see them on the waterline,
Sea dragons moving north to south.
Venus and Orion witness from afar.

Encinitas was so mesmerizing that I couldn't leave, as planned, to attend Wayne Dyer's public television taping of *The Shift: Taking One's Life from Ambition to Meaning*. I anchored in Encinitas.

Leaving my job opened ground for new possibilities and shook up a well-worn daily schedule. After eighteen years, I would now reach out in new directions, explore a wide range of job opportunities, meet new people, and learn new skills.

Different ground opened on January 30, 2009. Shaken out of a dreamy state at 5:30 a.m., television news confirmed a 4.5 earthquake. It's very humbling to feel Mother Earth shake the literal foundation that supports you, and to hear your house creak at the seams with the stress. Her unpredictable nature reminds us that we are not in control and, hopefully, makes us think of offering Her reverent gratitude. We are all in Her hands.

Will Mother Earth bring a new leveling field to all of us? Are we seeing just a glimpse of systems breaking down? Will we all be tested on survival? Not emotional survival or mental survival, but physical survival concerning basic needs: shelter, food, and water. Those of us unemployed begin to think about basic survival. It's a definite shift. Unemployment is like an earthquake with emotional waves high and low. It takes away an identity and leaves one without solid ground to stand on. I hear an anxious, worried voice say, "What about health insurance and the savings account?" My heart goes out to my extended unemployed family.

I never knew how driven I was—how much I pushed myself—never stopping to relax. Did I learn this from Mom, who raised six children and took little time for herself? Did I learn this from Dad, who was dedicated to his business and always busy hunting, fishing or playing basketball? Or did I learn this from a culture that encourages doing more, acquiring more—the faster the better?

I am *taking* a new look at this spinning pattern and putting the brakes on. I learn to live in the moment and not worry about the future. I learn to say "no" to this and "yes" to that. Simple activities make me happy, such as sewing a peace day banner for the upcoming International Day of Peace parade, reading about wild edible plants, and going into the nearby field to harvest nettle and dandelion.

Months after my job ended I took a deep breath and sensed a new quality of stillness. I was in the moment—relaxed! Anxiety had vanished and I was living without fear in the cycle of the unknown. Yes, I was now *being*. This "feminine" stillness deserves as much recognition as masculine achieving.

> Logical achieving is cold
> without emotional Being.

The part can never be well unless the whole is well.

—Plato

Chapter 30
Caduceus ~ A Story

For the first twenty-five years of my life, I was led by ego and then, thanks to the appearance of Archangel Michael, I was led by Light.

Light enlivens matter from atoms, cells, organs, bodies, and landmasses to moons, planets, and stars. In a dream at the end of 2013, I saw exactly how I am enlivened and led.

> I fly through space in one direction. A cord attached at the center top of my head pulls me another direction and then another. This gentle yet firm governance is sweet and I yield like a kite dancing in the wind—connected to Source.

Being led to a book on my bookshelf one morning, I turned the pages to an image of Caduceus and knew, in a flash, this as S/He Dragon! This speed-of-light seeing, and knowing the whole rather than the parts, is always a thrill, as if a dragon tail has just whipped through my field. This instantaneous seeing and knowing is why reading linear words feels tedious to me.

> *The caduceus is the traditional symbol of Hermes and features two snakes winding around an often winged*

staff. It is often mistakenly used as a symbol of medicine instead of the Rod of Asclepius, especially in the United States. The two-snake caduceus design has ancient and consistent associations with trade, eloquence, trickery, and negotiation. Tangential association of the caduceus with medicine has occurred through the ages, where it was sometimes associated with alchemy and wisdom.
—www.en.m.wikipedia.org/wiki/Caduceus_as_a_symbol_of_medicine

I saw beyond this left-brain information about the Caduceus and instinctually knew the image as a "story pole." The parts were communicating one whole S/He Dragon story. This is the story I saw and heard:

- Two serpents, (Sacred Feminine with negative (-) charge and Sacred Masculine with positive (+) charge), make contact, ignite, and combust, coiling around a spinal rod.

- Their honest communication and cooperation engage chakras, downloading from heaven and uploading from earth, a free-flowing current (-/+) of Kundalini life force.

- Life force activates wings of She and He—S/He—and circulates new vision in consciousness and new action in body.

- Two eyes, one attuned to heaven and one attuned to earth, sustain balance and equilibrium.

- Sacred Feminine and Sacred Masculine reveal the story pole, generating Light and Dark, delivering enlightenment.

S/He Dragon

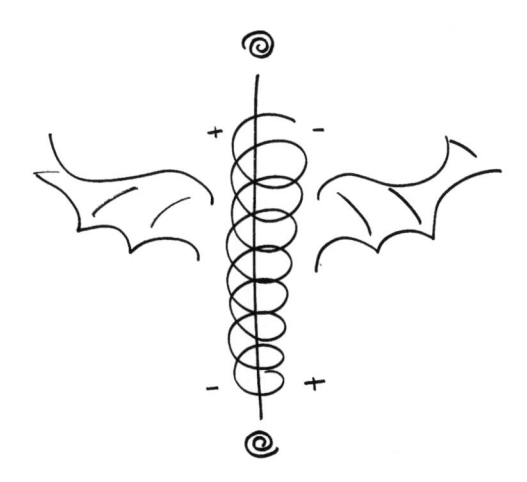

> Sacred Activism is the fusion of the mystic's passion for God with the activist's passion for justice, creating a third fire, which is the burning sacred heart that longs to help, preserve, and nurture every living thing.
>
> —Andrew Harvey

Chapter 31
Resilience ~ Blog 2010

This blog, written in 2010, reflects how I walk in diverse worlds. In hidden inner realms, I am Goddess, shaman, and mystic. In light of day, I am mother, grandmother, activist, teacher, and gardener. In writing this book and "coming out" as a mystic, will I be safe or ridiculed? The fact that those of us who see and hear differently are no longer burned at the stake gives testimony to new consciousness within humankind. This is a sign of hope... and safety.

Sacred Activism

I am a poet, writer, and visionary. I am more right-brained and intuitive than left-brained and logical. I need nature in order to breathe and thrive. I need land, trees, open space, and green valleys for inspiration, health, and well-being. For this reason, I am stepping into the mainstream political system to speak out for nature.

Profusion of Infusion

Earth is vibrating at a new frequency, spilling over in profuse color and delightful sound. These fairy dust particles, exuding through the parts and uplifting the whole, cannot be detected by five senses alone. Can this physical dimension continue to download this heavenly force? Change is inevitable.

Serpent's Forked Tongue

I woke up to serpent above my head, directly north, with forked tongue flicking. He was positioned west to east as a yogi appeared in white robe and sandals. What does this position on a circle communicate? I don't receive logical answers all at once so I listen and watch what shows up through ongoing moments of living. This trusting flow is the way of S/He Dragon.

> *Snakes don't sting or use their forked tongues as weapons. The tongues are perfectly harmless. A snake sticks out its tongue to collect data for its Jacobson's Organ, an organ strategically located in front of the roof of the snake's mouth that functions as a chemical receptor. For the male snake, the tongue is both a sensory organ, and a sensual organ. The tongue plays a vital role in snake courtship and reproduction, as the male snake's jerking body motions and rapidly flicking tongue either charm the female snake, or render her unresponsive. In either instance, by sticking out their tongues, snakes ensure the survival of the species.*
> —www.coolquiz.com/trivia/explain/docs/snakes.asp

Seeing Full Circle

I am learning more about my relationship with life force or prana. To learn is to turn within and listen. I am turning my head full circle like owl, seeing what's "behind" the scene of this "front" dimension. I see opening and movement in east/west relationship and circuitry. This morning as I was drumming and meditating, this turning to the back of the head created a headache. It's exercise to work new muscles and pathways involving Third-eye, Brain, and Body. I use capital letters with intention; this is sacred ground.

Sustainable Woodinville

I may be creating Sustainable Woodinville as an opportunity for local organizations to come together as a more integrated network. I want to make signs and organize a rally to protest the expansion of development around the valley where I live. What is my message? How do I deliver it? Will it create more borders and division?

Sacred activism, according to Andrew Harvey, Institute for Sacred Activism, (www.andrewharvey.net/sacred activism/), includes "profound spiritual and psychological self-awareness and deep truth, wisdom and compassion… the power of wisdom and love in action." This is the message I want to embrace and deliver and is a conversation to have as Sustainable Woodinville.

This is a vision, a seed. I've planted many seeds that did not sprout or bear fruit, but that doesn't stop this gardener. I forget the results. I never forget the joy of inspiration and its creativity.

Dr. Emoto's Salish Sea Blessing

Dr. Emoto, a Japanese author who claimed that human consciousness has an effect on the molecular structure of water, offered a sacred ceremonial blessing for Salish Sea and water everywhere at the Lummi Indian Nation Reservation near Bellingham, Washington. I eagerly carpooled with friends and joined many others on the beach as we blessed water, dedicating our sincere "prayer of love and gratitude to the water of Salish Sea and its rivers, and the waters of the world." Water was passed for everyone to bless and drink. Together, as one collective consciousness, we prayed, "Water, we are sorry. Water, we love you. Water, we thank you. Water, we respect you." It was an honor to meet Dr. Emoto, learn about the power of intention, and learn how exquisite water crystals manifest from positively charged words, music, and prayer.

Shamanic Pleat

An image of a skull and cross bones greeted my awakening eye. What force is projecting this image on my field of consciousness? I see with eyes at the back of my head and view "pleat" in the fabric, "split" in the mirror, or "splice" in the wire. Illusion of duality. We are shadow and light. In and out a revolving door that radiates and reflects. I don't make conclusions. I don't analyze. I don't question. I simply observe and blog so that I remember.

Mountaintop

I feel as if I am on top of a mountain. The air is new, as is my breathing. I see all around me in a 360-degree full circle. Relaxed, here and now, I apply for yet another job. Does one cycle end and another one begin? I have learned a lot about myself and others on this mountain. Here, I let go to flight. Now another mountain awaits.

The American Dream

I turned on CNN earlier today and heard an anchor talk about the American dream. He said the definition is a house, wealth, and materialism and added that this is not his dream, nor is it the dream of many others. He suggested that the American dream is changing.

Honey Bee Encounter

I worked in my garden yesterday, massaging soil and planting seeds. I was happy to see a honeybee in front of me, gathering pollen from the purple heal-all spilling profusely in every direction. Bees, associated with Goddess, were considered the souls of nymphs or priestesses who had been in the service of Aphrodite. I gave honeybee a burst of blessing for her part in the great circle of life. I dug dandelion roots to chop and roast for a nutritious coffee drink. Young nettles, carefully harvested, go into simmering soup on the stove—delicious! Wild foods' nutritional bounty has been forgotten by most people, which is why edible and medicinal plants are viewed as useless weeds.

It's Dragon Time

Last night's Sacred Feminine ritual was full of wonder and magic! I mentioned Dragon in a group of people I did not know and, surprisingly, met a man who has a "Dragon farm" in the area! He also teaches classes about Dragons. As we were talking, a large Dragon face appeared in the night sky, looking down at us. This Dragon's immensity reminded me of the mystical being I saw at Esalen Institute's shamanic workshop. This Dragon was red and gold. Another man, who is Asian, used a sword in the ritual, reminding me of Archangel Michael. Made by a Native American, the sword had dragons on the buffalo bone handle and sheath. Welcome, Dragon!

Dragon Speak

Dragon presence brings intensity and new activity as parts of my body "fuse." It's as if nerves and muscles are being stretched to new capacity. This development is part of an evolving process. Can this body hold the new vibration and charge? Of course! If not, this momentum would not be increasing. How does one manage the intensity of fire/heat? Moment by moment, through listening and responding. It's an ongoing learning process. Dragon Speak may not be understood by others. It is a different language, foreign to the left, logical brain. Dragon speak is instinctual, rising from ancient reptilian brain.

Gamma Rays

How are brainwaves associated with the ancient reptilian brain? Gamma brainwaves are not always acknowledged in the brainwave spectrum. I find them fascinating and sense they are part of S/He Dragon's flight.

Gamma brainwaves are the fastest brainwave frequency.

Neuroscientists believe that gamma waves are able to link information from all parts of the brain – the gamma wave originates in the thalamus and moves from the back of the brain to the front and back again 40 times per second—not only that, but the entire brain is influenced by the gamma wave. This rapid 'full sweep' action makes the gamma state one of peak mental and physical performance. Gamma is the brainwave state of being 'in the zone,' that feeling that you can do anything.
—www.omharmonics.com/blog/gamma-brain-waves/

Flying on dragon wings is a "gamma zone" experience!

Rooted Connection

My garden responds, giving me beans, potatoes, and mature ears of corn—my first corn crop! Witnessing the miraculous maturation process of root, stalk, leaf, ear, tassel, silk, cob, and kernel is fascinating. Is any other plant as wondrous as corn? Abundant tomatoes yield another batch of sauce. In spite of their greenery and blossoms, cucumbers and squash did not produce fruit. Is it lack of bees and thus, pollination?

At The Root Connection, Washington State's oldest community-supported agriculture (CSA) farm, I pick rainbow chard. In a moment of spontaneity, I ask Chard how I can ground and center as beautifully as she. The plant tells me to think of them and see them in their pink, red, yellow, and green veined leaves, rising up out of earth. By doing so, I will feel more grounded. Thank you, Chard! Time to dip my tomatoes into their hot water bath and dress them with onion, garlic, and basil. Yum!

Transition Summit

The Transition Summit was a regional gathering of seventy local participants focused on making communities more resilient in response to peak oil and climate change. I attended the "convergence" to learn how Transition Towns were different from Sustainable Cities. I met neighbors of like mind and heart, who lived five to 200 miles away, acting as catalysts to reduce their community's ecological footprint. Transition projects included planting a community garden, setting up a tool library, partnering with city government on a local Emergency Preparedness Plan, presenting "meaningful movies," and focusing on the "Heart and Soul" to address the inner dimensions of change. I was struck by the core values of the Transition Network: inclusion, hope, and "the creative genius" of community. Not only was this Transition network local, a national and international network was in place, and a handbook was available written by co-founder, Rob Hopkins. I felt new energy bursting forth in response to the challenges of our time. Transition had a song I wanted to sing, a dance I wanted to dance. I stepped out of that summit eager to organize Transition Woodinville.

Tools for Resilience

I am devouring *The Transition Handbook*, reading and highlighting it day and night—unheard of for one who has difficulty reading books that have myriad details about practical matters. This book is different, it weaves "head, heart and hands," one of Transition's slogans. I learn why we need to transition from peak oil and climate change, how we connect with others through the heart of inclusion, and what hands-on projects are already on the ground being implemented. This holistic model sold me on Transition and I wanted to include others in this "good news" about community resilience and sustainability.

City Council Drama

Our city is focused on development and many of us are concerned about big box stores coming into town. I spoke passionately at a city council about cities being built around the concept of happiness and referred to author Alain De Botton's book, *The Architect of Happiness*, (PantheonBooks/2006): "One of the great, but often unmentioned, causes of both happiness and misery is the quality of our environment: the kind of walls, chairs, buildings, and streets we're surrounded by."

There are a couple of council members who engage eye-to-eye when I speak; others turn away or look down. The vote was 4–2 in favor of less density. One local businessman was very upset by this unexpected outcome and called a council member "devious."

Transition Woodinville

At our Transition Woodinville orientation, I spontaneously opened the meeting by acknowledging our circle, the four directions, spirit beings, and angels holding these directions. This surprised me. These were not people I knew, and I am private about my spiritual work. However I flow with what is coming up from within, in the moment. I trust this process and the group appeared to be comfortable with it. We agreed to have a discussion group focusing on *The Transition Handbook*.

City Council Talk, November 9

"I represent Transition Woodinville locally and Transition Towns globally. Our focus is to build resilient communities in this time of critical change. As you, Woodinville City Council, move forward in a business-as-usual reality, supporting growth and development, Transition Woodinville moves forward in a different reality supporting sustainability and doing more with less. How can we bridge the two?

Transition Towns address issues of

- Peak oil—advocating for energy descent action plans.
- Climate change—advocating for localization and community resilience.
- Food scarcity—advocating for local farms and organic gardens.
- Economic instability—advocating for new systems of local exchange."

Dream Time

Shimmering golden serpent rises from underground in vibrant green habitat. Very regal. S/he is facing east with a section of body pulsating above the ground. When I awoke, I understood this was its heart. I also saw a blue serpent in the same upright position facing east. Do these vibrant images communicate increased life force? As I awoke from another dream, I saw myself getting out of a white "cab." This tickled me. Am I chauffeured in and out of dreamtime?

Surround Sound

I wear a cloud of ascension taking me away from earth's dense matter.

I try to focus and stay grounded in thoughts, tasks, and responsibilities.

However, surround-sound frequency lifts me and I float in subtle, energetic space.

Inner Transition

In our final Transition discussion group, we discussed how our lives had changed during the series. One woman said that she was off antidepressants; another no longer felt alone; and another expressed gratitude for her eighty-year-old father who taught her skills, such as beekeeping, wild edible plant identification, fermentation and canning. This inner heart and soul of transition is where true change happens. Personal transition, from the inside out, ensures that we are not engaged in politics as usual.

May Queen

In stillness, a hazy face appeared in a mystical windowpane shimmering with green vining leaves and violet-blue flowers. When I attempted to draw her face, I couldn't. She was too ethereal. She definitely had two soft eyes. She beckoned me to go out the window with her, so I did. We journeyed. She seems familiar and I sense I've seen her in a book about fairies. I think of the May Queen (also known as the flower bride, queen of the fairies, and the lady of the flowers) in association with all the plants/shrubs/trees that are budding out around my little house and in my valley—in December!

> Shamanic journeying is the inner art of traveling to the invisible worlds beyond ordinary reality to retrieve information for change in any area of your life—from spirituality and health to work and relationships.
>
> —Sandra Ingerman, *Shamanic Journeying*

Chapter 32

Soul Retrieval

I crack open my egg shell and emerge from an inner cave. For over forty years I listened and moved with the rhythms of sunrise and sunset as Light and Dark nudged me onward and upward. Now out of shell and cave, my wings are dry. This is no flying dream. This is earth plane reality as I tell my story in the eyes and ears of the public. My intention is to assist others in bringing sacred Light to life on planet Earth, on Gaia.

S/He Dragon, my ongoing spiritual journey, is a process of reaching for Light. Like a seed I am drawn out of the dark soil. "Grow, grow, grow!" is the command of Light. From sprout to stem, stem to bud, bud to leaf, leaf to flower, and flower to fruit I develop, fulfilling an inherent design to be all that I can be. Each stage of development provides an opportunity to simply "be." A sprout doesn't want to be a stem. It is too busy sprouting. A leaf doesn't want to be a flower. It is too busy leafing. Step by step, focused within, each stage of growth adds substance to the whole process of spiritual development.

Light has positive, life-affirming qualities. Instead of depression I find rapture; instead of grief I find joy; instead of loneliness I find comfort in Nature; instead of being alone I find a worldwide network of people making their communities more local—people-and-earth-friendly. This enlightening process unfolds me organically: moment by moment, day by day, year by year, and lifetime by lifetime.

Negative emotions, thoughts, and actions reveal the absence of Light and reflect lost soul parts in one's psyche. To go within and retrieve these lost parts requires humility. Facing the traumas, addressing the wounds is the warrior's journey that involves more than the mental (beta brainwave frequency) mind. Doing so requires the focus of personal commitment. To build new neurons in the brain-body and expand one's range of brainwave frequencies is deep spiritual work. The opportunity is evolutionary! Through conscious choice the Angel-Human can recover what has been lost and forgotten.

We lost Her way of seeing and didn't know where to find Her. We turned away from Her instinctual, holistic knowing toward a fast-paced life-style with material values, scientific scrutiny and dissection, and technological worship. Her absence represents half of our intelligence and this absence is evident as personal well-being falters, interpersonal relationships wobble, and as social, economic, political, and ecological systems fall into chaos. In this crisis of loss, personally and collectively, we have the opportunity to remember our whole and holy selves through soul retrieval. We remember this for ourselves, as planetary citizens, and for Gaia.

Ozone warms, waters rise, whales beach.
Frogs deform, fruits freeze, bees vanish.
Soil erodes, seeds alter, trees die.
Is it too late to save ourselves?

Fear controls, anger enrages, addiction enslaves.
Despair limits, depression darkens, abuse damages.

Resentment poisons, rage frightens, violence destroys.
Is it too late to save ourselves?

Shift fear to love, anger to peace, addiction to freedom.
Shift despair to hope, depression to joy, abuse to caring.
Shift resentment to forgiveness, rage to resolution, violence to peace.
Shift inner environment and save ourselves!

Soul retrieval reintegrates parts of oneself that might have been disconnected, lost, or trapped through trauma. At Esalen Institute in Big Sur, California, I joined a group of shamans to practice soul retrieval for Mother Earth. "Shamanism is a practice that involves a practitioner reaching altered states of consciousness in order to encounter and interact with the spirit world and channel these transcendental energies into this world." (www.en.m.wikipedia.org/wiki/Shamanism)

Trish Blog —Shamanic Journey, Esalen

> Fire lifts me into expansive cosmic space. I see Jupiter's rings. One has a beam of dark, manipulative energy directed toward earth. I put my right hand out demanding this interference stop. I sense white cotton between human ears and find this comical. It's time to recharge the parts between the ears, the brain. The retrieval of soul parts awakens the human brain and the global brain of Gaia. Horses come into view—horsepower!

I drew images of this shamanic journey in my journal. Soon after, a staff photographer spoke about rock art and then shared photographs, informing us that Esalen Indians had lived in the area 7,000 years earlier. The petroglyph images were similar to those I had drawn in my journal: a tall shaman with head in the cosmos and one hand visible. The difference was my shaman had curves—a *shawoman!* I imaged/

imagined her curves on rock, joining a lineage of healers, creating a new petroglyph for past, present, and future.

When I shared some of my Esalen experiences with a friend she commented that I could now tell her how I "do" shamanism. My response was quick, without thought. "I don't do shamanism. Shamanism does me." As these words spontaneously rose up from the underground of unconsciousness and out my mouth, I witnessed their meaning. Shamanism is not something I learn or do through my mental mind. Shamanism is something I am: receptive, attuned, aligned in altered states of consciousness. Not when I want or need to be shamanic. Not something I turn on and off. But something that moves through me spontaneously, purely, without analytical interference.

I prefer letting my instinctual/reptilian brain-body teach me experientially, rather than learning about shamanism from a book or teacher. This form of inner knowing, however, is not acknowledged in this world of achievement with its official certificates and degrees. Education, for me, means going to books, and listening to experts, *after* I have personal experience and have generated substance within my own experience. This is simply the way I have been guided, the way my life has unfolded.

Here is another example of how shamanism "does me."

In the middle of the night, I thought of a woman friend who is deeply depressed due to rejection by a man. I reached out to her and found myself shaking a rattle above her head to clear out toxic, negative patterns. The rattling reverberated loudly in shamanic space/time.

Where did this rattle come from? I had not intended it, nor thought about it previously. I was simply a vessel letting spirit move through me. This "instinctual" response is letting go to spirit and letting the intelligence of Light fill in the space of emotion, mind and body. There is nothing more thrilling than to yield and watch what falls into place.

...The Life Force has a sound (though ordinarily it is inaudible) because it is essentially movement and movement is what produces sound. The life force "pulsates" like a heart-beat or the regular, monotonous rhythm of a drum, and it also "vibrates," swirling and spiraling in flowing, circular motions like seeds swishing in a rattle when it is shaken. So a drum and a rattle in the hands of a shamanist are not simply means of making a noise, however joyful, but also means of simulating the sound and movement of the Life Force. This is why the drum and the rattle are principal tools of the shaman.
—Author Kenneth Meadows, *Where Eagles Fly: A Shamanic Way to Inner Wisdom*/EarthQuest/1995

Rattles have revealed themselves as medicine for my journey, and I say "thank you."

Imagine yourself holding a shamanic rattle. Listen to it reverberate, activating the electromagnetic life force in and around you. Now imagine this life force extending outward and around the planet. Feel your oneness with the Earth, with Gaia, as She turns from the dark night into the morning sun's embrace. Greet the solar sun as it feeds your spiritual eye and energetic body and your physical eyes and material body. Sense this yielding to Light and being infused with the glory of dawn. Feel yourself as Mother Earth, as Gaia, turning toward Light of a new day, and kissed by dawn's gifts of inspiration, information, and images. In this brainwave frequency, between dark and dawn, let your inner shaman out into expression.

One morning an unfriendly face appeared in my mind's eye, the third-eye chakra. This was not the first unfriendly face I had seen that week and both had one thing in common: demonic eyes. One other face I perceived had no eyes, so, with mischievous enthusiasm, I energetically added two that sparkled with life. I am a spiritual activist and whenever

I sense a negative entity or force in my energetic field I counter with something positive. Often it is humorous and lighthearted—the best way to dissipate negativity.

An artist friend visited me one day and painted a wolf; I painted a flower. She showed me a portrait she had sketched from a previous incident when she was in bed, noticed movement on the covers, and saw a menacing face. Petrified, she could not move, so she prayed. A white light appeared in the corner of her room and expanded. When it dissipated, the intruder was gone. Months later she traveled to Iowa to visit her daughter and showed her the portrait. Her daughter jumped up and left the room to return with a portrait she had sketched—of the same Shadow Man!

There was a distinct feature in the sketched face that reminded me of a news story about the Sandy Hook Elementary School shooting in Newton, Connecticut on December 14, 2012. The shooter had the same look in his eyes as 'shadow man": demonic.

It's time to expose evil entities, invisible to most people. Intuitive seers and shamans sense and often see these behind-the-scenes forces that support demonic behavior. When the unfriendly face appeared that morning, my hand and rattle went directly in front of his face. Again, this automatic, instinctual response is why I don't do shamanism and how shamanism does me. My guidance is within. I am receptive and flow with this innate intelligence, yielding myself as a shamanic tool, and receiving tools as needed. This instinctual knowing means yielding oneself in the spontaneity of the moment, as Light moves through matter.

Trish Blog —Shamanic Tools

> I awoke to Shadow Man's face in the distance and through mind's eye spontaneously lifted my right arm,

sprinkling him with sparkling fairy dust from a wand. I asked how a fairy wand is different from a rattle. The answer: they are similar energetically, both an extension of one's hand that radiates healing rays.

When a one-eyed cyclops' face appeared, I spontaneously gestured toward him with a wand. He didn't vanish, so I tapped him directly on the head. "Thunk!" I actually felt something solid in etheric space! Later, thinking about a friend, I felt a vibrational connection and my right hand spontaneously reached out and... touched her... hand to hand! So fun! So loving!

Trish Blog —Be Not Afraid

Yesterday morning when I awoke, sword spoke (representing Archangel Michael), showing that its blade "point" is positioned south, its "grip" north, and the "cross guard" is east and west. Through intuition's direct knowing I "got" that sword is to be released in a "ritual." This information was accompanied by a wind chime tone. The ritual involved lifting the sword up and out of earth. I saw cracks opening and golden Light pouring forth. Then I saw sword lying on the ground in a mystical grotto. The sword was horizontal and radiating golden rays... ley lines. "Be not afraid" came in.

Celtic Knot

In the space between dark of night and light of dawn, I saw, through third-eye, a serpent moving as a Celtic knot, black with yellow stripe. Soon after, a grabbing hand shot up from southeast. I didn't understand the meanings so I radiated Light. The next morning, I awoke after a stressful dream and knew: There are forces trying to destroy the Sacred Feminine.

The Celtic knot symbol is also referred to as the mystic knot, or the endless knot. The more esoteric or spiritual meaning of this symbol eludes to beginnings and endings. In viewing these beautiful knots, we cannot see a beginning or an end and therefore we are reminded of the timeless nature of our spirit. This translation harkens to our most primal selves as we contemplate the infinite cycles of birth and rebirth in both physical and ethereal realms.
—www.whats-your-sign.com/celtic-knots.html

I live in two worlds. One is mystical, and the other is down to earth. Both worlds contain a vast number of moving parts of which I, physical form/Matter and spiritual energy/Light, am one. What is the purpose of meeting and greeting as parts of one whole? What is the purpose of crossing paths? For me the answer is simple: the evolution of matter through the enlightenment of human consciousness.

Enlightenment is knowing my Dark body with its shadowy reflections and my Light body with its spiritual radiance. My material body is grounded in Earth, ever evolving and finite, while my spiritual body is infinite, aligned with the cosmos. One supports the other, breathing together through expansion and contraction in an evolving journey of grace.

> To see what was hidden is to unlock a secret code.
> To wrap what was behind with what is in
> front is to break hypnotic spell.
> To find within what is lost without is retrieval of soul.
> To join as One, is flying on wings.